The Best of Drawn and quarterly

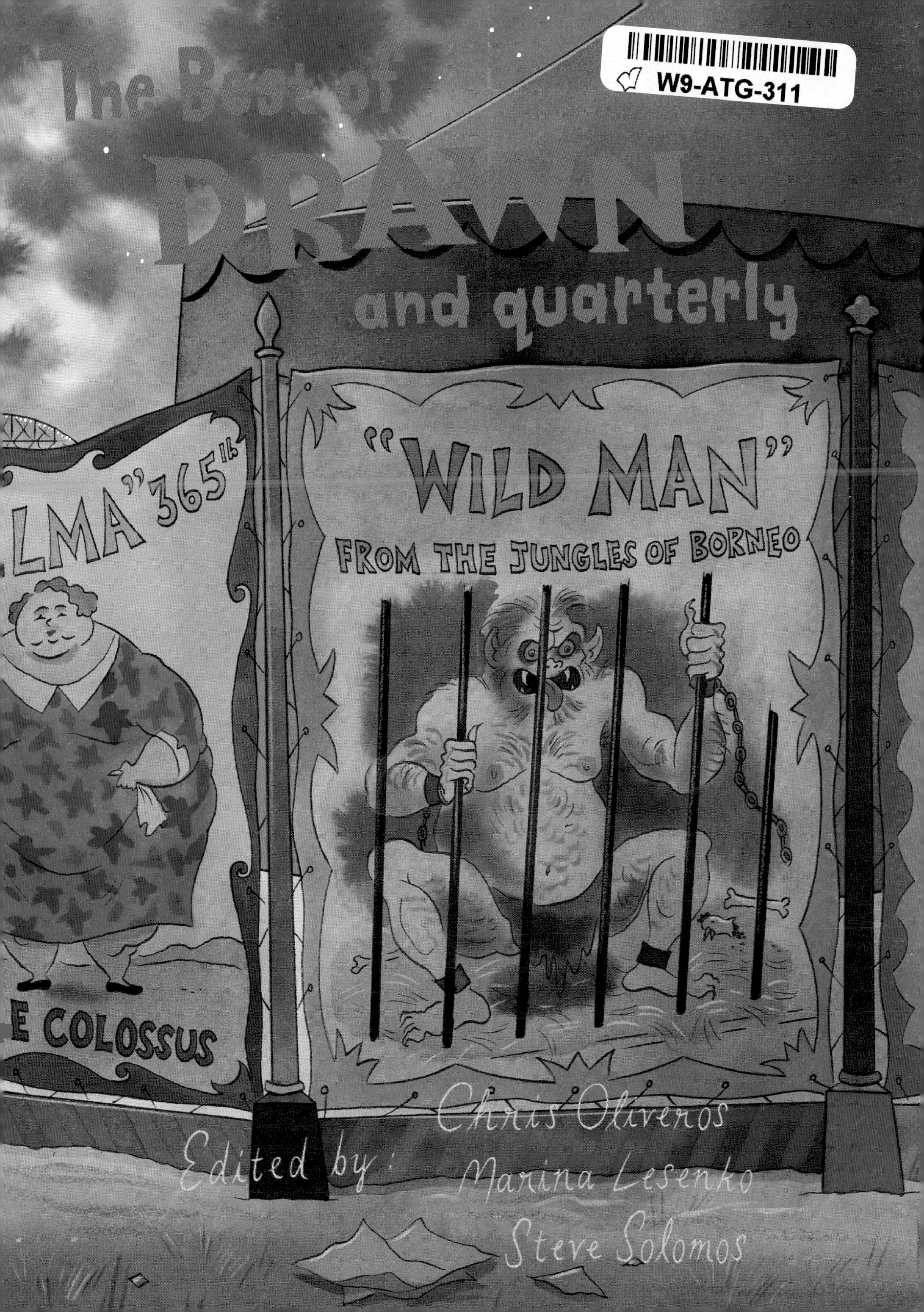

"WILD MAN"
FROM THE JUNGLES OF BORNEO
LMA" 365^{lb}
E COLOSSUS

Edited by: Chris Oliveros
Marina Lesenko
Steve Solomos

I give thanks to the Holly Saint of the Miracles and the Virgin of the Sacred Thoughts for helping me when I needed them most and the alligator who believed in my convictions.
April 23 1974
John Kapinsky.

Introduction by Peter Bagge

About four years ago I got a phone call from a young, ambitious, Peter Lorré-sound-a-like named Chris Oliveros, who wanted to pick my brain regarding what was then, and still is, a sore subject with me. Apparently this Montreal-based art school graduate got this foolish notion in his noggin that what he wanted to do more than anything else in the whole wide world was publish and edit a regular "alternative comix" anthology. I, having attempted similar ventures in the past, assured him that this would be a big mistake; that to edit such a title has to be the most thankless task in the world, but seeing his mind was made up, I gave him a few "helpful hints", wished him a lot of much needed luck, and awaited word of his giving up in complete despair.

Since that time Chris has put out (with the editorial help, later on, of Marina Lesenko and Steve Solomos) ten issues of *Drawn & Quarterly*, as well as a line of six regular comic titles that have followed it, and boy am I impressed! Not only has *Drawn & Quarterly* been a consistently satisfying read during its entire run, but the afore-mentioned off-shoot titles: *Dangle, Dirty Plotte, Palooka-Ville, Peep Show, Slutburger,* and *Yummy Fur* make up the most consistent, high-quality imprint I have ever known of. There quite simply isn't a clunker in the bunch!

The "secret" to Oliveros' success is due mainly to the fact that he chooses the artists he uses very carefully. A high percentage of them are already established professional illustrators (Seth, Drechsler, Vellekoop, King, Moiseiwitsch, Kuper, Sala, Mazzucchelli, Cohen), which help give *Drawn & Quarterly* a sophisticated, almost *New Yorker*-ish feel to it. The stories also tend to reflect those that you'll come across in classic literary magazines, from "southern gothic" (Dougan), to urban neurotic (Matt). Couple this with its high production values, and one would think *Drawn & Quarterly* would be the ideal "cross-over" title, one that appeals to that ever-elusive non-comic-buying (as in non-superhero-loving) public, a goal that this collection is at least partially designed to achieve. Again, due to past experience I remain pessimistic in this regard, but Chris Oliveros has proven me wrong before, so here's hoping he does it again. And if this book *does* make the NY Times Best-Sellers list, remember this: You heard it here first!

- Peter Bagge,
Seattle, December 1993

The Best of Drawn & Quarterly. ISBN 0-9696701-4-1. Edited by Chris Oliveros, Marina Lesenko, and Steve Solomos. Covers and endpapers by Maurice Vellekoop. Published by Drawn & Quarterly Publications; Chris Oliveros and Marina Lesenko: Publishers. Entire contents ©Copyright 1993 Drawn & Quarterly Publications. Stories and art ©Copyright 1993 by the respective artists. All rights reserved. For a list of other fine comics and books published by D&Q write for our free mail order catalogue: Drawn & Quarterly Publications, 5550 Jeanne Mance Street, #16, Montreal, Quebec, Canada H2V 4K6. PRINTED IN HONG KONG. First Printing: December 1993.

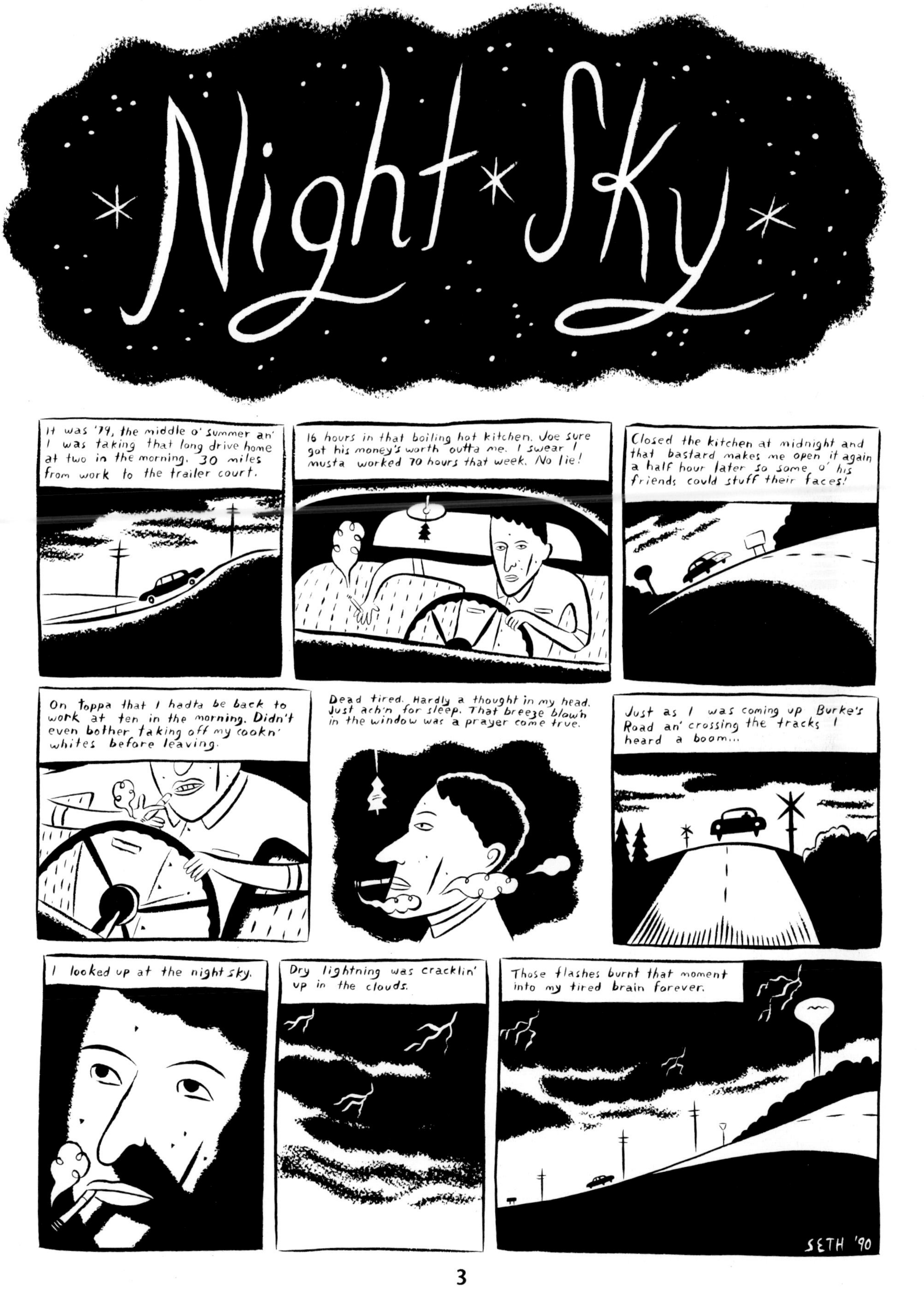
Night Sky
It was '74, the middle o' summer an' I was taking that long drive home at two in the morning. 30 miles from work to the trailer court.
16 hours in that boiling hot kitchen. Joe sure got his money's worth outta me. I swear I musta worked 70 hours that week. No lie!
Closed the kitchen at midnight and that bastard makes me open it again a half hour later so some o' his friends could stuff their faces!
On toppa that I hadta be back to work at ten in the morning. Didn't even bother taking off my cookn' whites before leaving.
Dead tired. Hardly a thought in my head. Just ach'n for sleep. That breeze blow'n in the window was a prayer come true.
Just as I was coming up Burke's Road an' crossing the tracks I heard a boom...
I looked up at the night sky.
Dry lightning was cracklin' up in the clouds.
Those flashes burnt that moment into my tired brain forever.
SETH '90

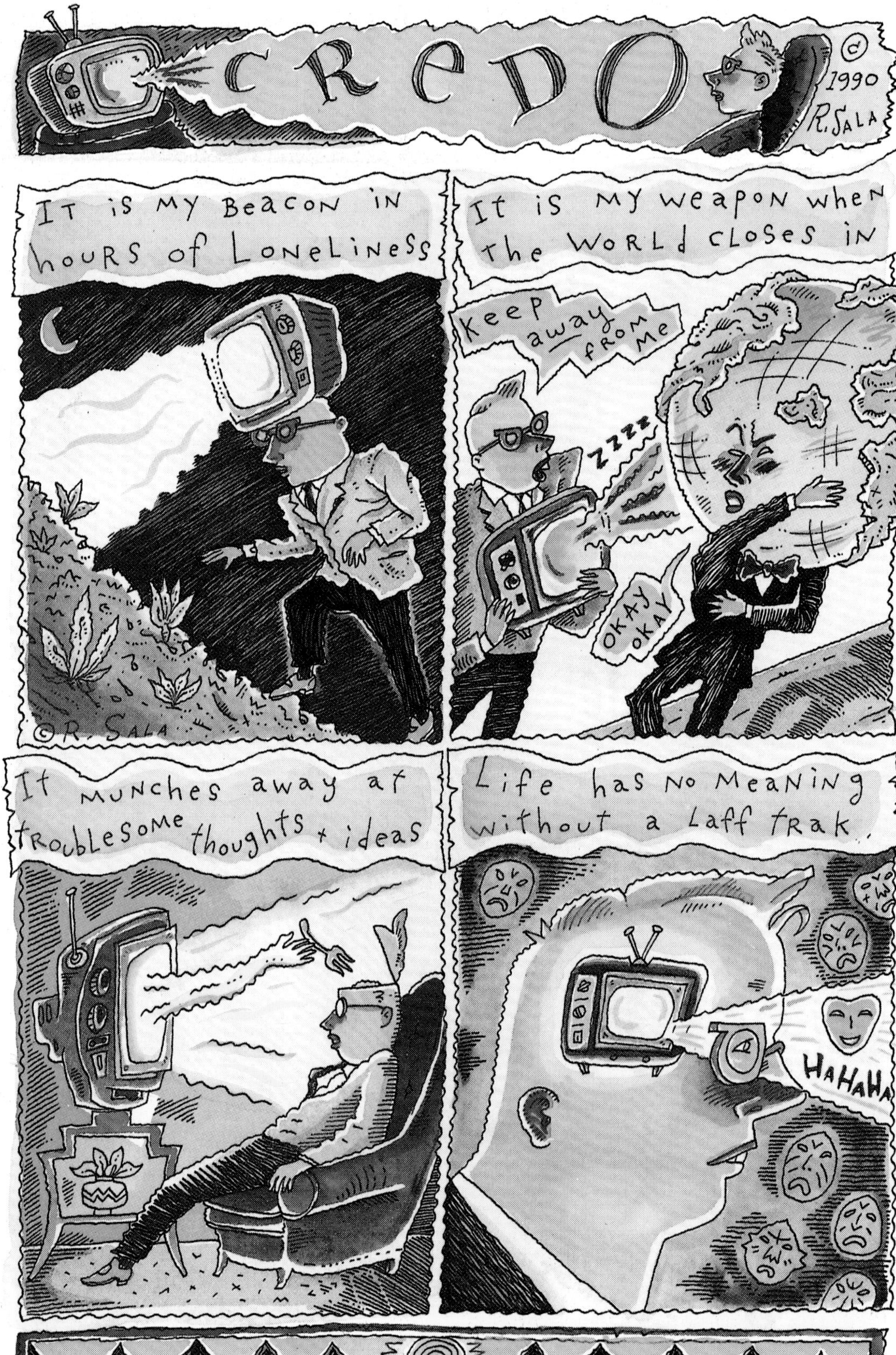
CREDO
© 1990 R. SALA
It is my beacon in hours of loneliness
©R. SALA
It is my weapon when the world closes in
Keep away from me
ZZZZ
OKAY OKAY
It munches away at troublesome thoughts + ideas
Life has no meaning without a laff trak.
HaHaHa

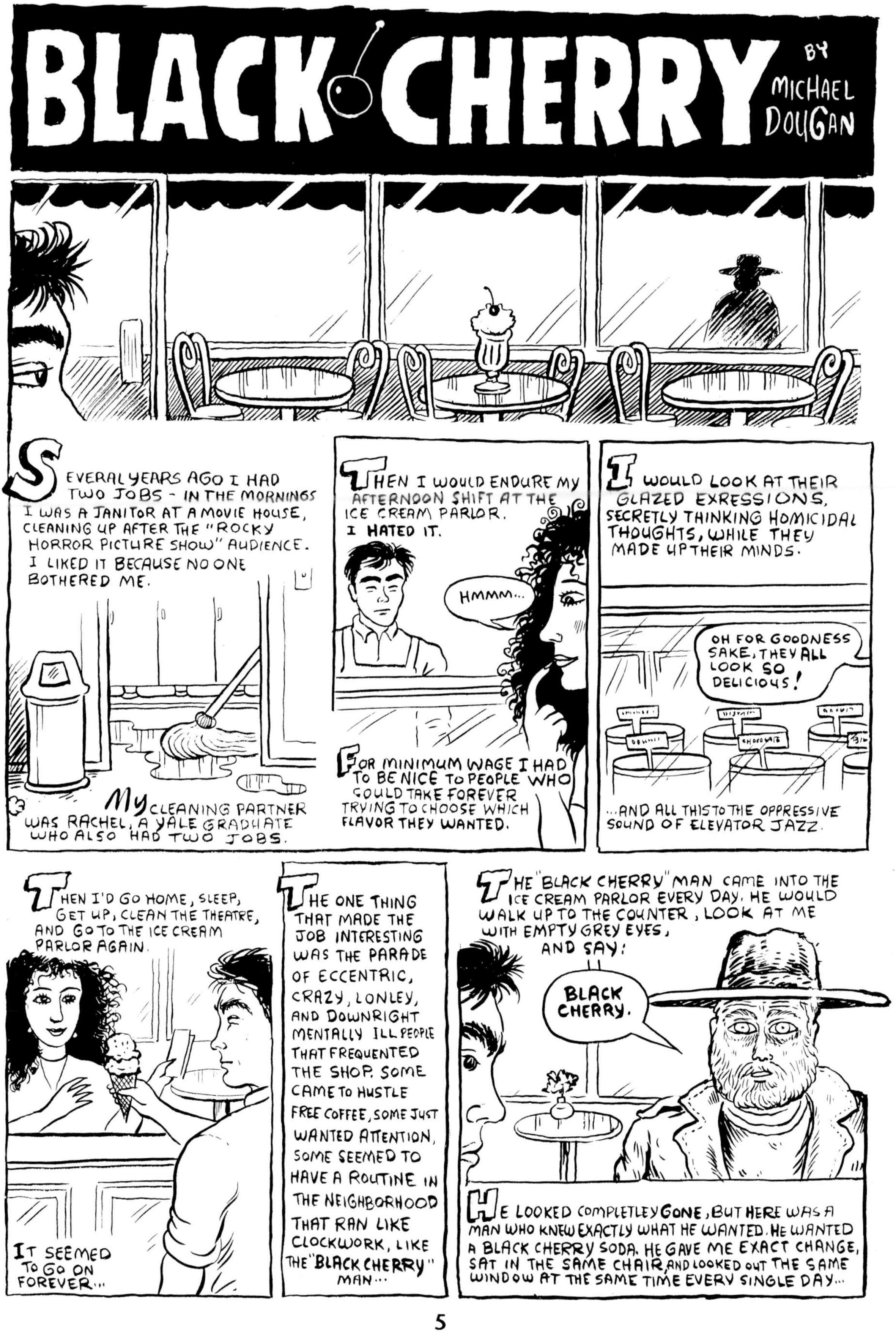
BLACK CHERRY
BY MICHAEL DOUGAN
SEVERAL YEARS AGO I HAD TWO JOBS - IN THE MORNINGS I WAS A JANITOR AT A MOVIE HOUSE, CLEANING UP AFTER THE "ROCKY HORROR PICTURE SHOW" AUDIENCE. I LIKED IT BECAUSE NO ONE BOTHERED ME.
MY CLEANING PARTNER WAS RACHEL, A YALE GRADUATE WHO ALSO HAD TWO JOBS.
THEN I WOULD ENDURE MY AFTERNOON SHIFT AT THE ICE CREAM PARLOR. I HATED IT.
HMMM...
FOR MINIMUM WAGE I HAD TO BE NICE TO PEOPLE WHO COULD TAKE FOREVER TRYING TO CHOOSE WHICH FLAVOR THEY WANTED.
I WOULD LOOK AT THEIR GLAZED EXRESSIONS, SECRETLY THINKING HOMICIDAL THOUGHTS, WHILE THEY MADE UP THEIR MINDS.
OH FOR GOODNESS SAKE, THEY ALL LOOK SO DELICIOUS!
...AND ALL THIS TO THE OPPRESSIVE SOUND OF ELEVATOR JAZZ.
THEN I'D GO HOME, SLEEP, GET UP, CLEAN THE THEATRE, AND GO TO THE ICE CREAM PARLOR AGAIN.
IT SEEMED TO GO ON FOREVER...
THE ONE THING THAT MADE THE JOB INTERESTING WAS THE PARADE OF ECCENTRIC, CRAZY, LONLEY, AND DOWNRIGHT MENTALLY ILL PEOPLE THAT FREQUENTED THE SHOP. SOME CAME TO HUSTLE FREE COFFEE, SOME JUST WANTED ATTENTION, SOME SEEMED TO HAVE A ROUTINE IN THE NEIGHBORHOOD THAT RAN LIKE CLOCKWORK, LIKE THE "BLACK CHERRY" MAN...
THE "BLACK CHERRY" MAN CAME INTO THE ICE CREAM PARLOR EVERY DAY. HE WOULD WALK UP TO THE COUNTER, LOOK AT ME WITH EMPTY GREY EYES, AND SAY:
BLACK CHERRY.
HE LOOKED COMPLETLEY GONE, BUT HERE WAS A MAN WHO KNEW EXACTLY WHAT HE WANTED. HE WANTED A BLACK CHERRY SODA. HE GAVE ME EXACT CHANGE, SAT IN THE SAME CHAIR, AND LOOKED OUT THE SAME WINDOW AT THE SAME TIME EVERY SINGLE DAY...

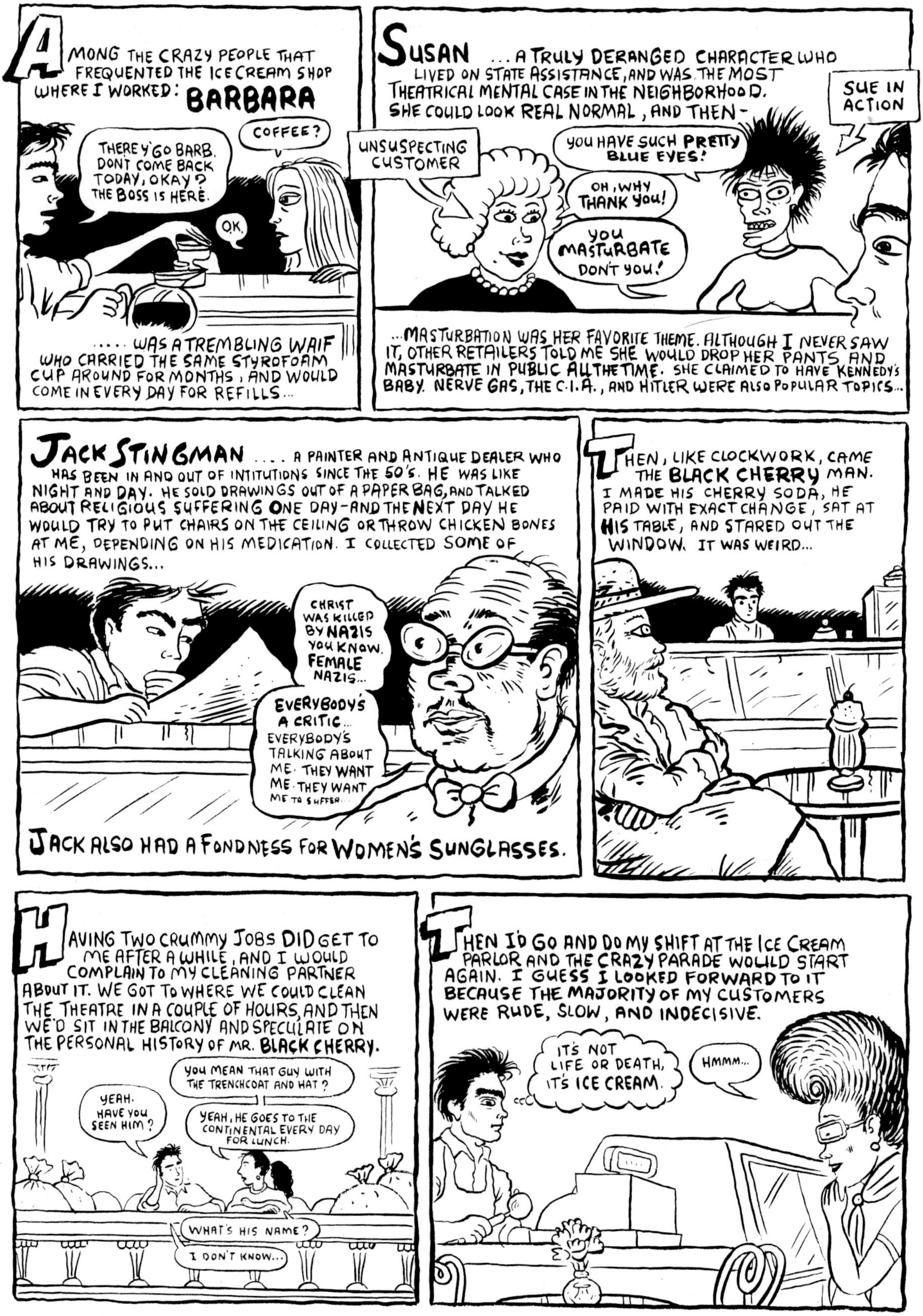
AMONG THE CRAZY PEOPLE THAT FREQUENTED THE ICE CREAM SHOP WHERE I WORKED: BARBARA
THERE Y'GO BARB. DON'T COME BACK TODAY, OKAY? THE BOSS IS HERE.
COFFEE?
OK.
.... WAS A TREMBLING WAIF WHO CARRIED THE SAME STYROFOAM CUP AROUND FOR MONTHS, AND WOULD COME IN EVERY DAY FOR REFILLS...
SUSAN ... A TRULY DERANGED CHARACTER WHO LIVED ON STATE ASSISTANCE, AND WAS THE MOST THEATRICAL MENTAL CASE IN THE NEIGHBORHOOD. SHE COULD LOOK REAL NORMAL, AND THEN -
UNSUSPECTING CUSTOMER
SUE IN ACTION
YOU HAVE SUCH PRETTY BLUE EYES!
OH, WHY THANK YOU!
YOU MASTURBATE DON'T YOU!
...MASTURBATION WAS HER FAVORITE THEME. ALTHOUGH I NEVER SAW IT, OTHER RETAILERS TOLD ME SHE WOULD DROP HER PANTS AND MASTURBATE IN PUBLIC ALL THE TIME. SHE CLAIMED TO HAVE KENNEDY'S BABY. NERVE GAS, THE C.I.A., AND HITLER WERE ALSO POPULAR TOPICS...
JACK STINGMAN .... A PAINTER AND ANTIQUE DEALER WHO HAS BEEN IN AND OUT OF INTITUTIONS SINCE THE 50'S. HE WAS LIKE NIGHT AND DAY. HE SOLD DRAWINGS OUT OF A PAPER BAG, AND TALKED ABOUT RELIGIOUS SUFFERING ONE DAY - AND THE NEXT DAY HE WOULD TRY TO PUT CHAIRS ON THE CEILING OR THROW CHICKEN BONES AT ME, DEPENDING ON HIS MEDICATION. I COLLECTED SOME OF HIS DRAWINGS...
CHRIST WAS KILLED BY NAZIS YOU KNOW, FEMALE NAZIS...
EVERYBODY'S A CRITIC... EVERYBODY'S TALKING ABOUT ME. THEY WANT ME. THEY WANT ME TO SUFFER...
JACK ALSO HAD A FONDNESS FOR WOMEN'S SUNGLASSES.
THEN, LIKE CLOCKWORK, CAME THE BLACK CHERRY MAN. I MADE HIS CHERRY SODA, HE PAID WITH EXACT CHANGE, SAT AT HIS TABLE, AND STARED OUT THE WINDOW. IT WAS WEIRD...
HAVING TWO CRUMMY JOBS DID GET TO ME AFTER A WHILE, AND I WOULD COMPLAIN TO MY CLEANING PARTNER ABOUT IT. WE GOT TO WHERE WE COULD CLEAN THE THEATRE IN A COUPLE OF HOURS, AND THEN WE'D SIT IN THE BALCONY AND SPECULATE ON THE PERSONAL HISTORY OF MR. BLACK CHERRY.
YEAH. HAVE YOU SEEN HIM?
YOU MEAN THAT GUY WITH THE TRENCHCOAT AND HAT?
YEAH, HE GOES TO THE CONTINENTAL EVERY DAY FOR LUNCH.
WHAT'S HIS NAME?
I DON'T KNOW...
THEN I'D GO AND DO MY SHIFT AT THE ICE CREAM PARLOR AND THE CRAZY PARADE WOULD START AGAIN. I GUESS I LOOKED FORWARD TO IT BECAUSE THE MAJORITY OF MY CUSTOMERS WERE RUDE, SLOW, AND INDECISIVE.
IT'S NOT LIFE OR DEATH, IT'S ICE CREAM.
HMMM...

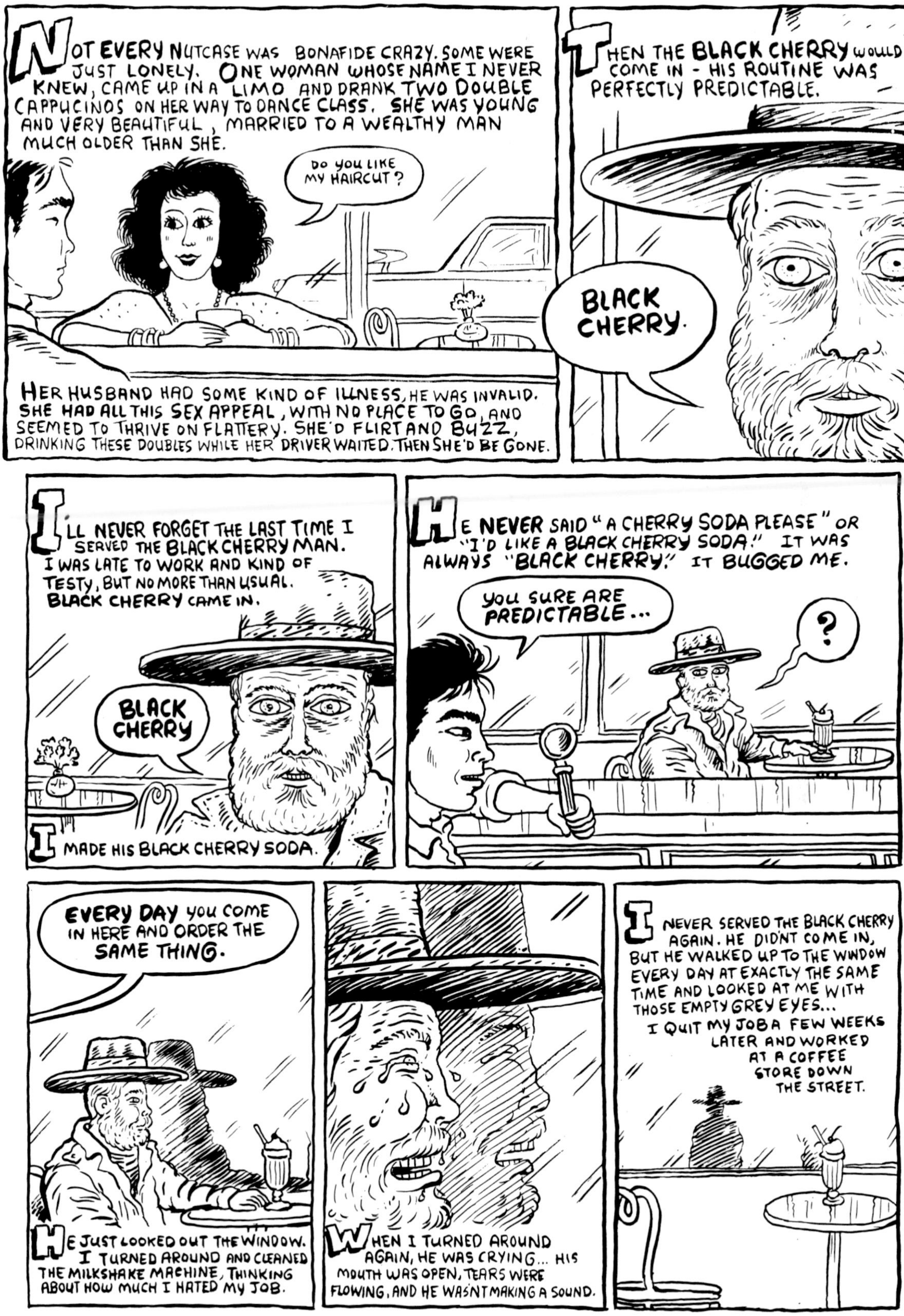
NOT EVERY NUTCASE WAS BONAFIDE CRAZY. SOME WERE JUST LONELY. ONE WOMAN WHOSE NAME I NEVER KNEW, CAME UP IN A LIMO AND DRANK TWO DOUBLE CAPPUCINOS ON HER WAY TO DANCE CLASS. SHE WAS YOUNG AND VERY BEAUTIFUL, MARRIED TO A WEALTHY MAN MUCH OLDER THAN SHE.
DO YOU LIKE MY HAIRCUT?
HER HUSBAND HAD SOME KIND OF ILLNESS, HE WAS INVALID. SHE HAD ALL THIS SEX APPEAL, WITH NO PLACE TO GO, AND SEEMED TO THRIVE ON FLATTERY. SHE'D FLIRT AND BUZZ, DRINKING THESE DOUBLES WHILE HER DRIVER WAITED. THEN SHE'D BE GONE.
THEN THE BLACK CHERRY WOULD COME IN - HIS ROUTINE WAS PERFECTLY PREDICTABLE.
BLACK CHERRY.
I'LL NEVER FORGET THE LAST TIME I SERVED THE BLACK CHERRY MAN. I WAS LATE TO WORK AND KIND OF TESTY, BUT NO MORE THAN USUAL. BLACK CHERRY CAME IN.
BLACK CHERRY
I MADE HIS BLACK CHERRY SODA.
HE NEVER SAID "A CHERRY SODA PLEASE" OR "I'D LIKE A BLACK CHERRY SODA." IT WAS ALWAYS "BLACK CHERRY." IT BUGGED ME.
YOU SURE ARE PREDICTABLE...
?
EVERY DAY YOU COME IN HERE AND ORDER THE SAME THING.
HE JUST LOOKED OUT THE WINDOW. I TURNED AROUND AND CLEANED THE MILKSHAKE MACHINE, THINKING ABOUT HOW MUCH I HATED MY JOB.
WHEN I TURNED AROUND AGAIN, HE WAS CRYING... HIS MOUTH WAS OPEN, TEARS WERE FLOWING, AND HE WASN'T MAKING A SOUND.
I NEVER SERVED THE BLACK CHERRY AGAIN. HE DIDN'T COME IN, BUT HE WALKED UP TO THE WINDOW EVERY DAY AT EXACTLY THE SAME TIME AND LOOKED AT ME WITH THOSE EMPTY GREY EYES... I QUIT MY JOB A FEW WEEKS LATER AND WORKED AT A COFFEE STORE DOWN THE STREET.

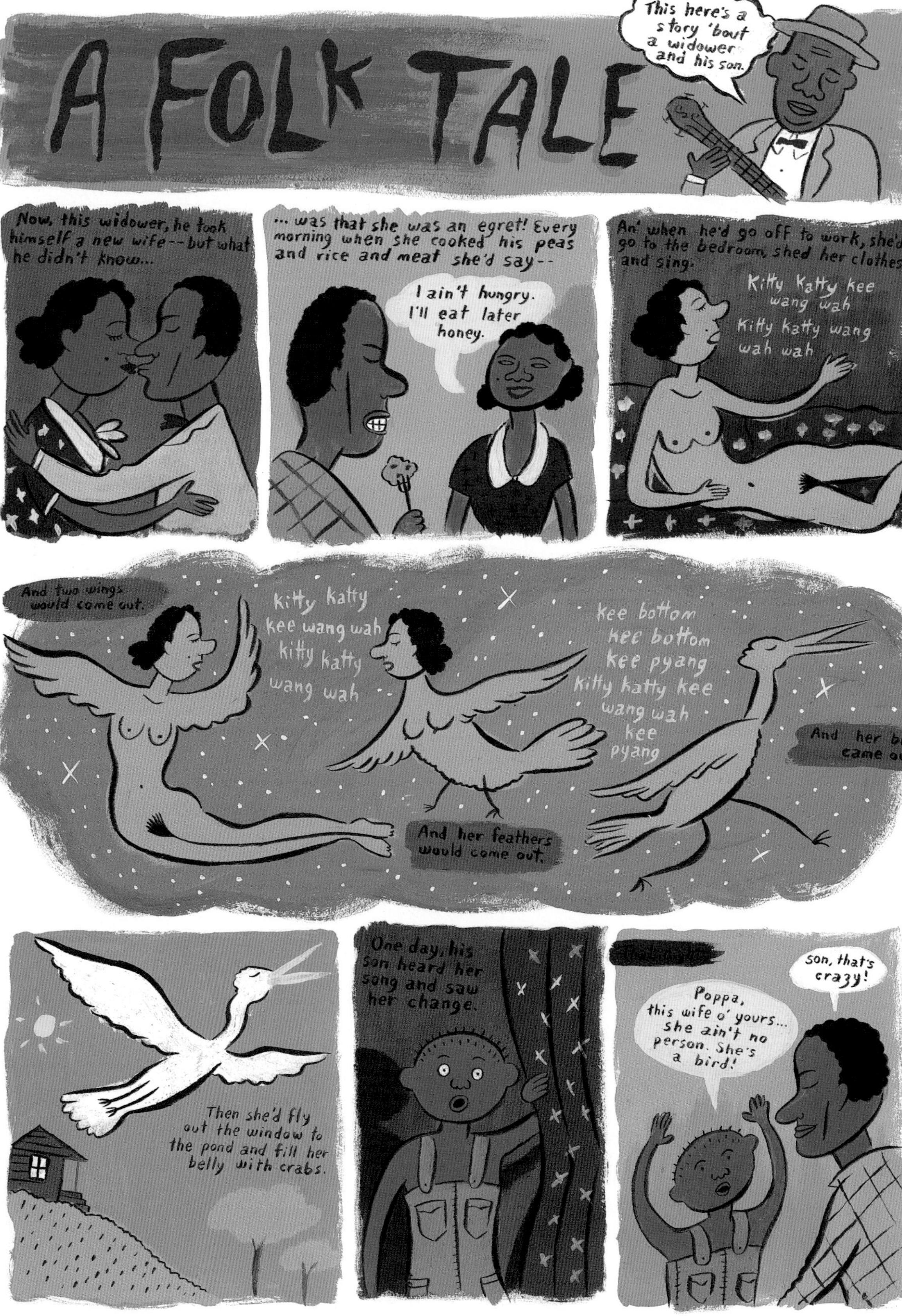
A FOLK TALE
This here's a story 'bout a widower and his son.
Now, this widower, he took himself a new wife -- but what he didn't know...
... was that she was an egret! Every morning when she cooked his peas and rice and meat she'd say --
I ain't hungry. I'll eat later honey.
An' when he'd go off to work, she'd go to the bedroom, shed her clothes and sing.
Kitty Katty kee wang wah
Kitty katty wang wah wah
And two wings would come out.
kitty katty kee wang wah kitty katty wang wah
And her feathers would come out.
kee bottom kee bottom kee pyang kitty katty kee wang wah kee pyang
And her bill came out.
Then she'd fly out the window to the pond and fill her belly with crabs.
One day, his son heard her song and saw her change.
[redacted]
Poppa, this wife o' yours... she ain't no person. She's a bird!
son, that's crazy!

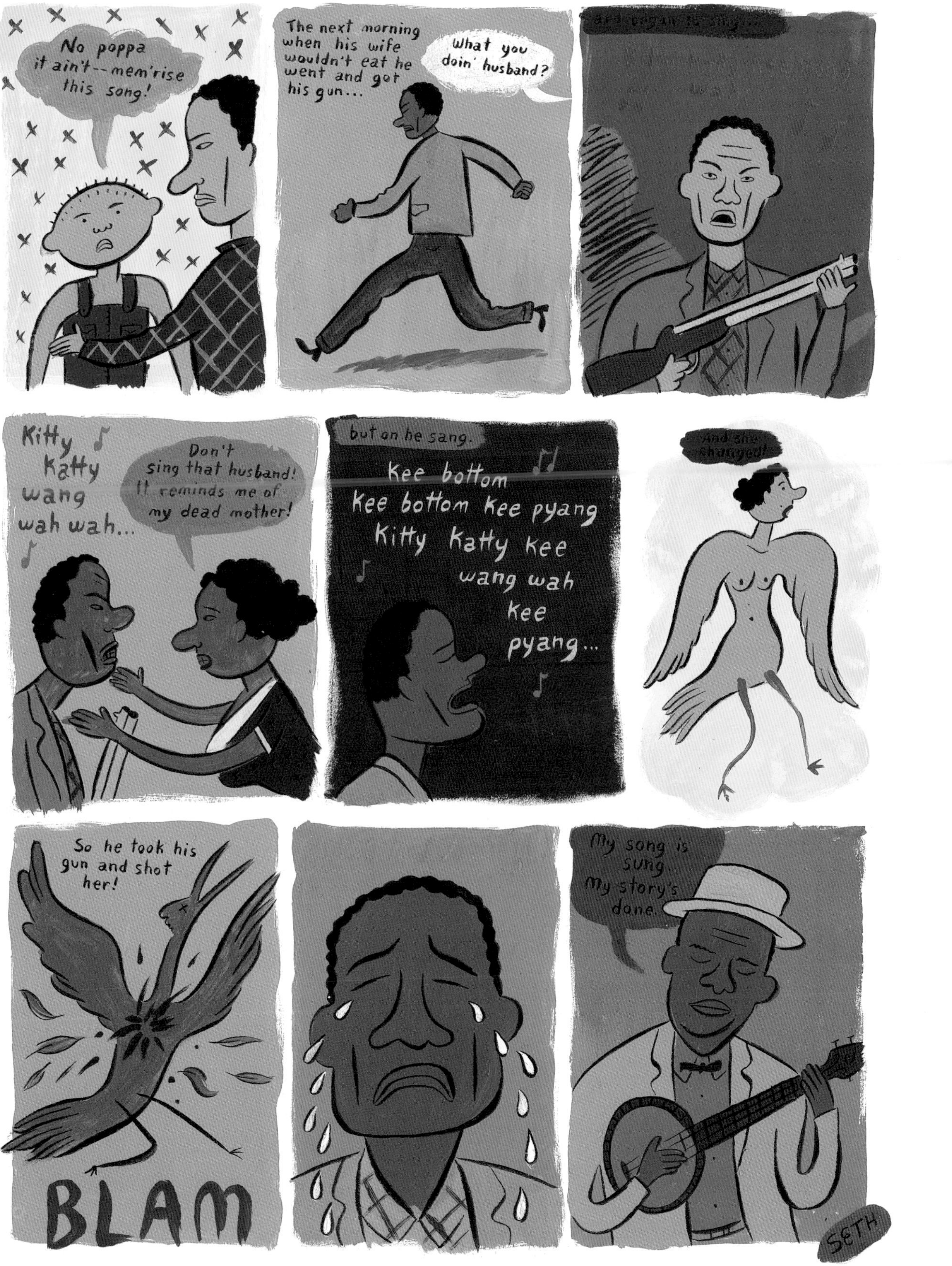
No poppa it ain't-- mem'rise this song!
The next morning when his wife wouldn't eat he went and got his gun...
What you doin' husband?
and began to sing...
Kitty Katty wang wah wah...
Don't sing that husband! It reminds me of my dead mother!
but on he sang.
Kee bottom kee bottom kee pyang Kitty Katty kee wang wah kee pyang...
And she changed!
So he took his gun and shot her!
BLAM
My song is sung. My story's done.
SETH

8 Pillars of Gay Culture

hand-written by Doctor Maurice "Vivienne" Vellekoop, Bachelor. ©1991

1 ANCIENT GREECE

The wonderful world of Ancient Greece, where men loved boys, exerts a lifelong fascination for homosexuals, no matter how they're introduced to it.

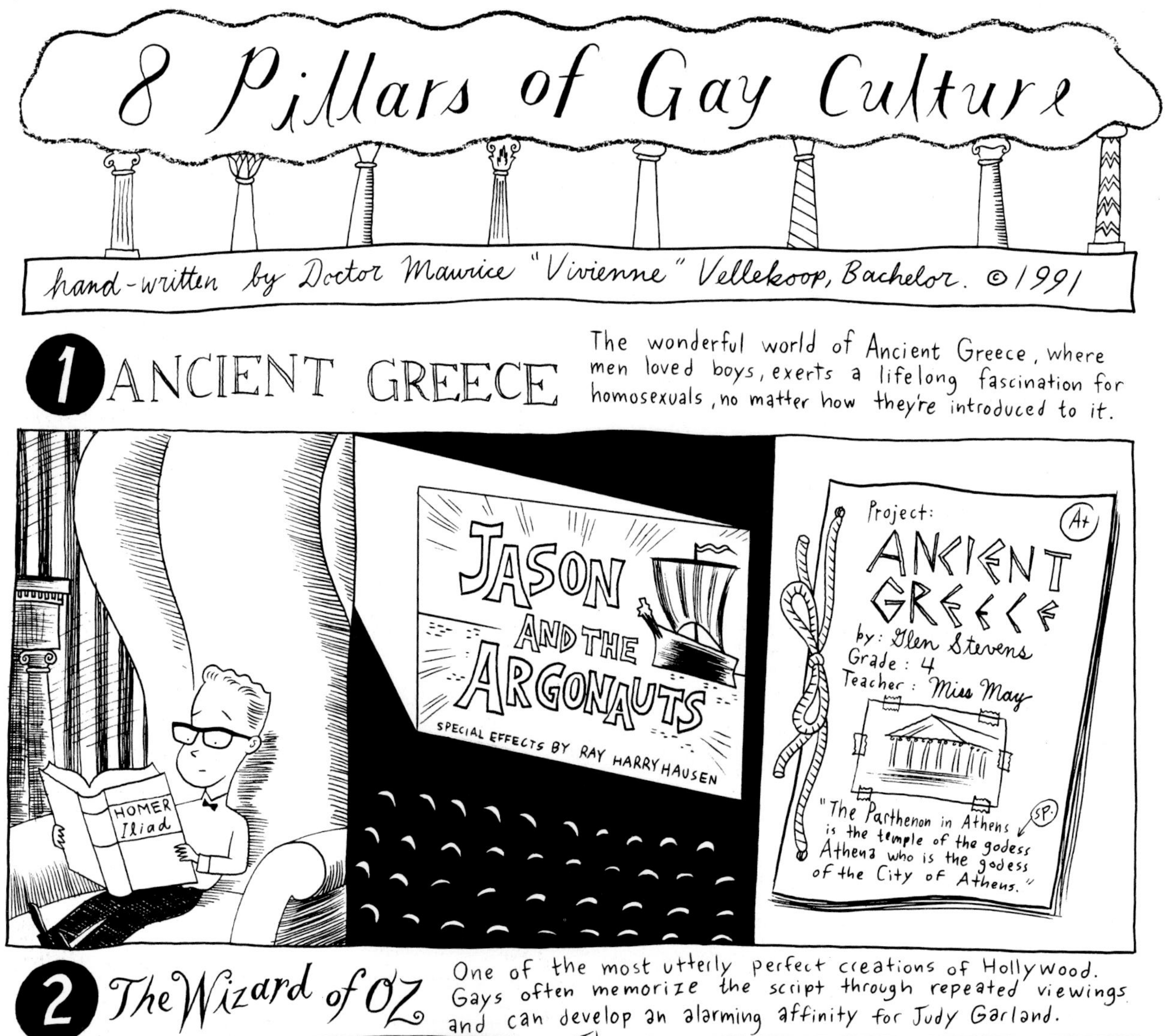

HOMER
Iliad
JASON AND THE ARGONAUTS
SPECIAL EFFECTS BY RAY HARRYHAUSEN
Project:
A+
ANCIENT GREECE
by: Glen Stevens
Grade: 4
Teacher: Miss May
"The Parthenon in Athens is the temple of the godess Athena who is the godess of the City of Athens."
SP.

2 The Wizard of OZ

One of the most utterly perfect creations of Hollywood. Gays often memorize the script through repeated viewings and can develop an alarming affinity for Judy Garland.

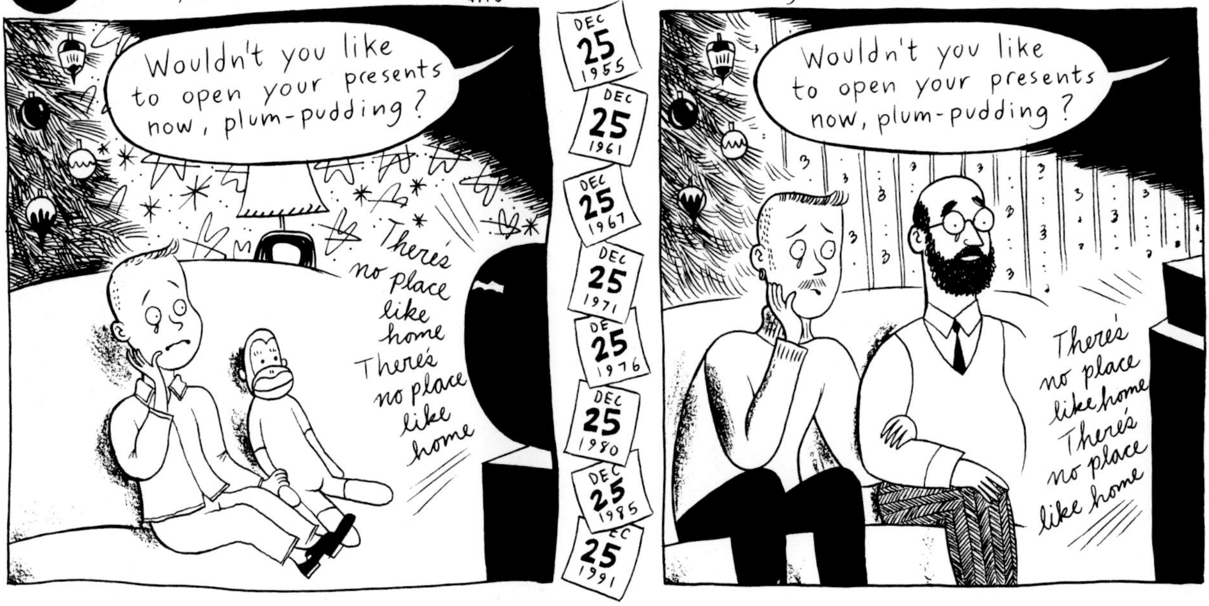

Wouldn't you like to open your presents now, plum-pudding?
There's no place like home There's no place like home
DEC 25 1955
DEC 25 1961
DEC 25 1967
DEC 25 1971
DEC 25 1976
DEC 25 1980
DEC 25 1985
DEC 25 1991
Wouldn't you like to open your presents now, plum-pudding?
There's no place like home There's no place like home

3 Oscar Wilde

Surely Wilde represents the first true flowering of a gay sensibility both in his art and life. His epigrams come in handy in any situation.

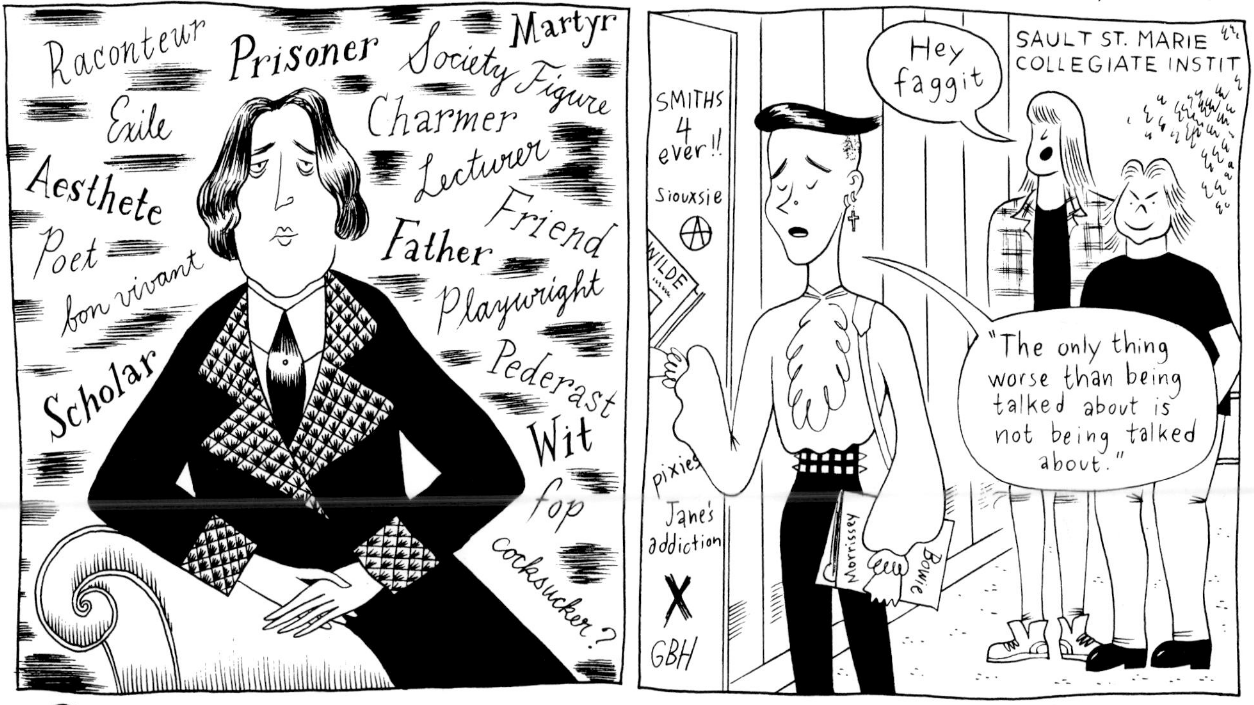

Raconteur
Prisoner
Society Figure
Martyr
Exile
Charmer
Aesthete
Lecturer
Poet
Friend
Father
bon vivant
Playwright
Scholar
Pederast
Wit
fop
cocksucker?
SMITHS 4 ever!!
Siouxsie
WILDE
pixies
Jane's addiction
X
GBH
Morrissey
Bowie
Hey faggit
SAULT ST. MARIE COLLEGIATE INSTIT
"The only thing worse than being talked about is not being talked about."

4 Style

Beauty, Perfection, fashion, decoration, taste and extravagance are the traditional realms of the homosexual.

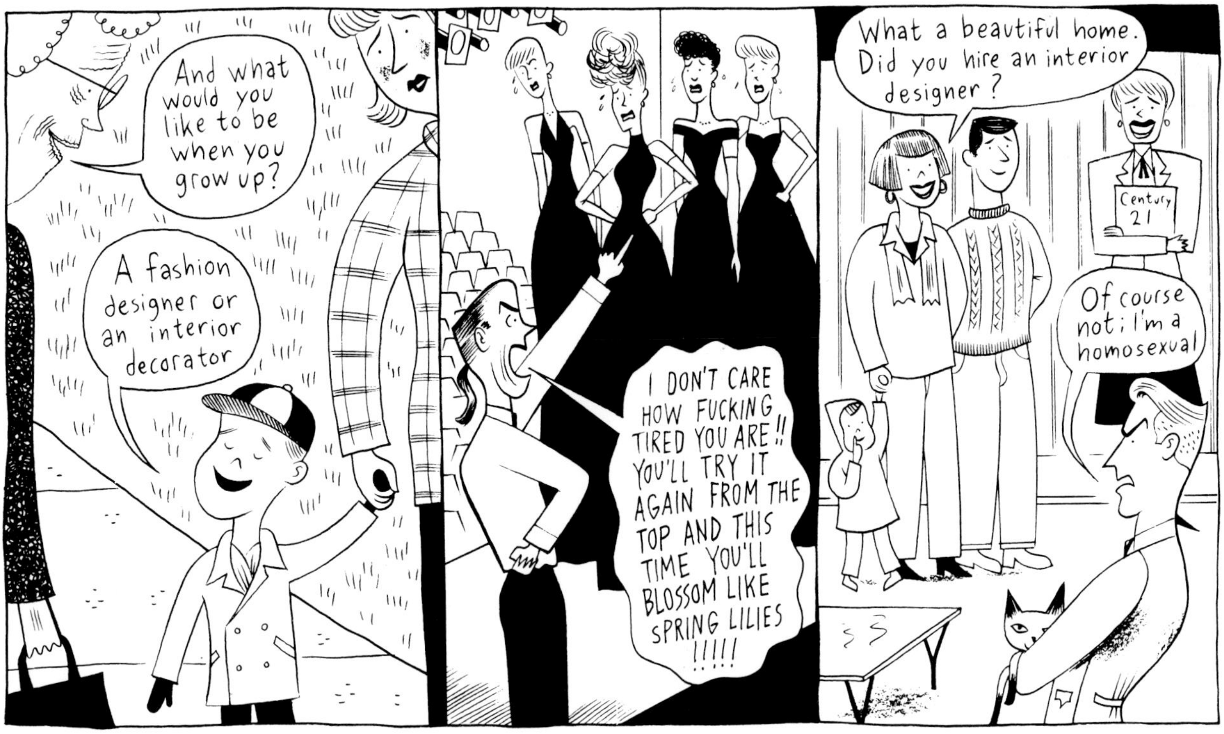

And what would you like to be when you grow up?
A fashion designer or an interior decorator
I DON'T CARE HOW FUCKING TIRED YOU ARE!! YOU'LL TRY IT AGAIN FROM THE TOP AND THIS TIME YOU'LL BLOSSOM LIKE SPRING LILIES !!!!!
What a beautiful home. Did you hire an interior designer?
Century 21
Of course not; I'm a homosexual

5 Swan Lake

This work, so removed from everyday life, with its themes of longing and loss, has a very emotional pull for gays. Though they may have seen one too many productions, these jaded queens respond deep down with genuine affection to its romantic beauty.

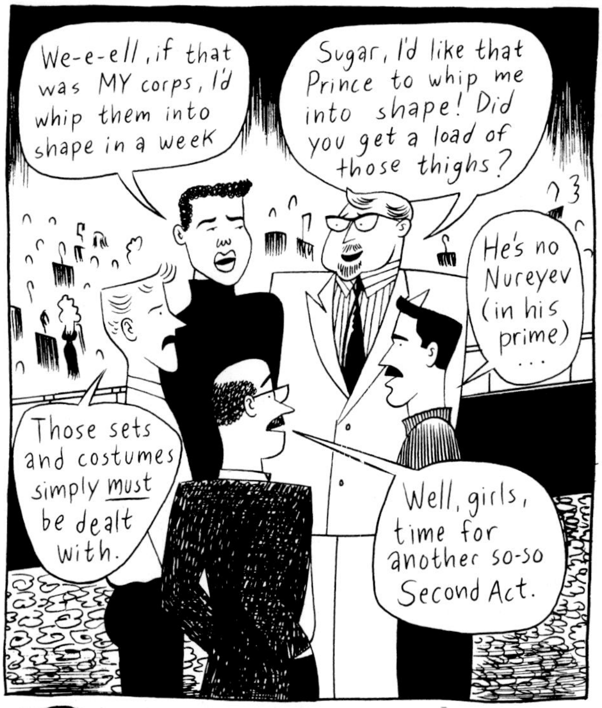

We-e-ell, if that was MY corps, I'd whip them into shape in a week
Sugar, I'd like that Prince to whip me into shape! Did you get a load of those thighs?
He's no Nureyev (in his prime) ...
Those sets and costumes simply must be dealt with.
Well, girls, time for another so-so Second Act.

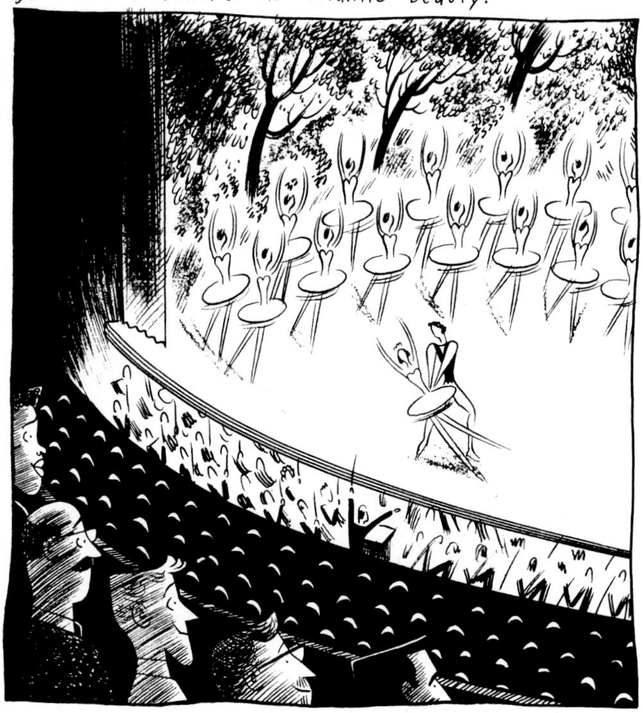

6 La Traviata

Stories of beautiful women who suffer, sacrifice and die find a home in the hearts of gays. Surely Violetta suffers the most poignantly. Her dilemma, whether to party carelessly or fall in love and risk getting hurt, is every gay man's dilemma.

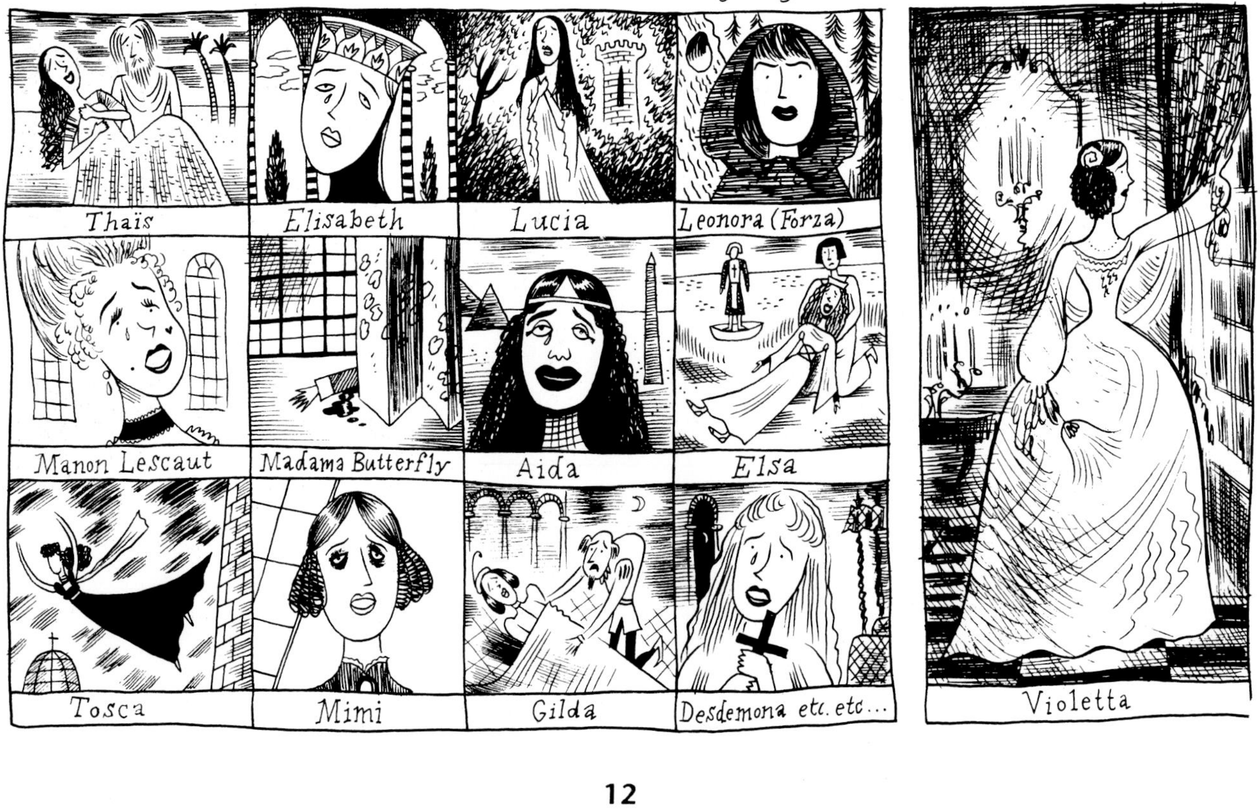

Thaïs
Elisabeth
Lucia
Leonora (Forza)
Manon Lescaut
Madama Butterfly
Aida
Elsa
Tosca
Mimi
Gilda
Desdemona etc. etc...
Violetta

7 Sunset Boulevard

Gays identify with dark, grotesque figures like Norma Desmond, Blanche Dubois and Baby Jane Hudson. The antitheses of the "good" 19th-century heroines, they are just as much victims; of a hard, callous society and their own minds.

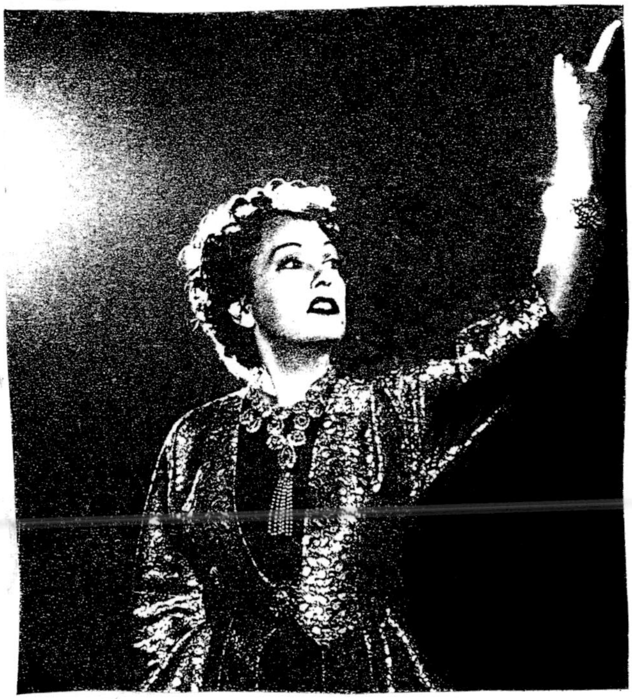

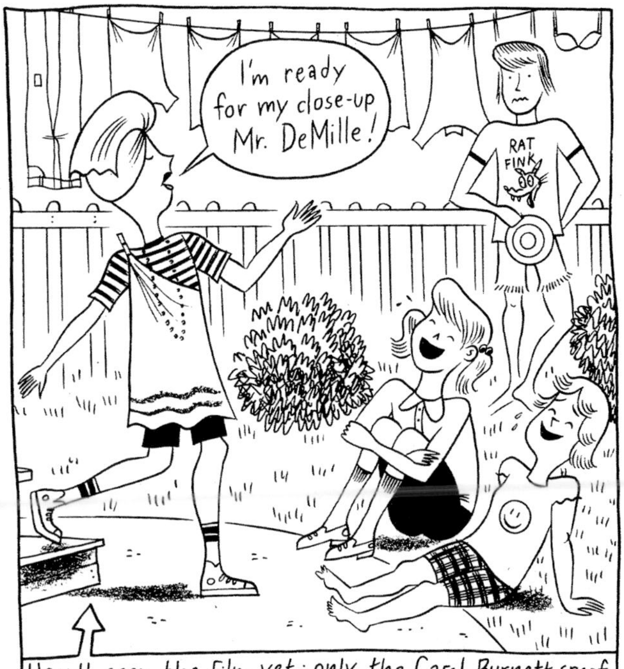
I'm ready for my close-up Mr. DeMille!
RAT FINK
Hasn't seen the film yet; only the Carol Burnett spoof.

8 What Ever Happened to Baby Jane?

If camp was a bicycle, Bette Davis and this film would be the training wheels. Davis is arguably the greatest movie star ever.

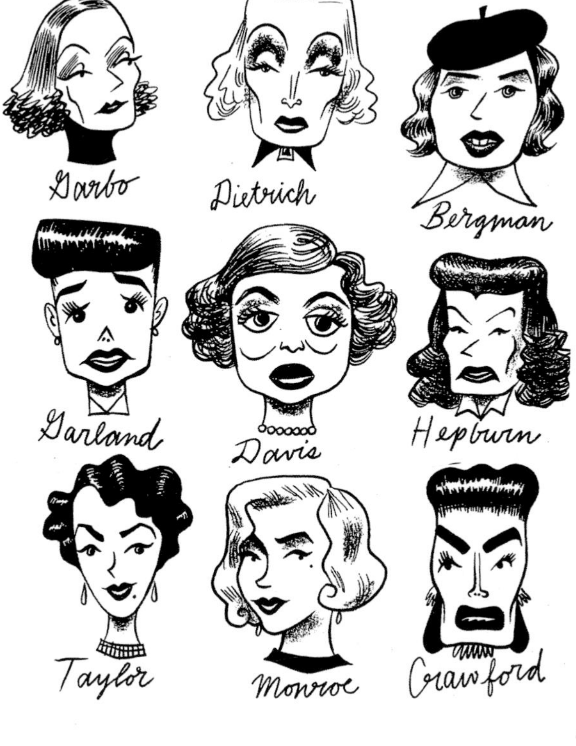
Garbo
Dietrich
Bergman
Garland
Davis
Hepburn
Taylor
Monroe
Crawford

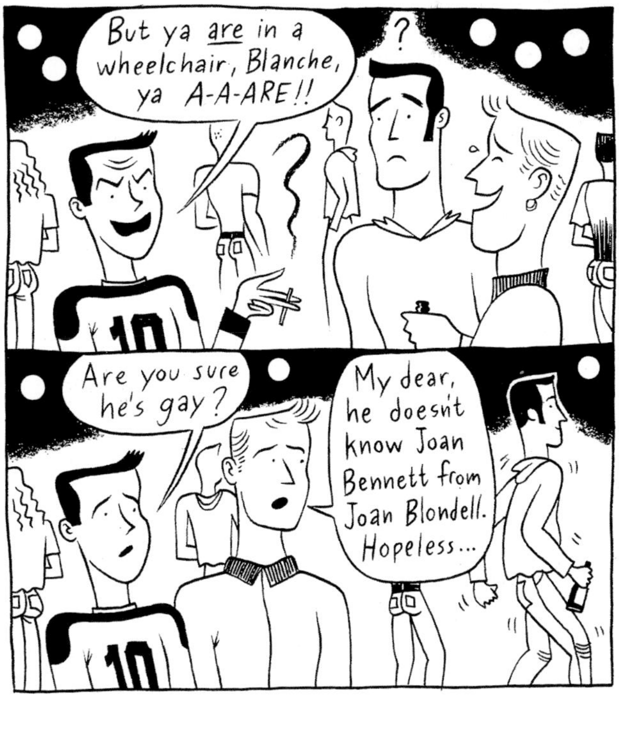
But ya are in a wheelchair, Blanche, ya A-A-ARE!!
?
Are you sure he's gay?
My dear, he doesn't know Joan Bennett from Joan Blondell. Hopeless...

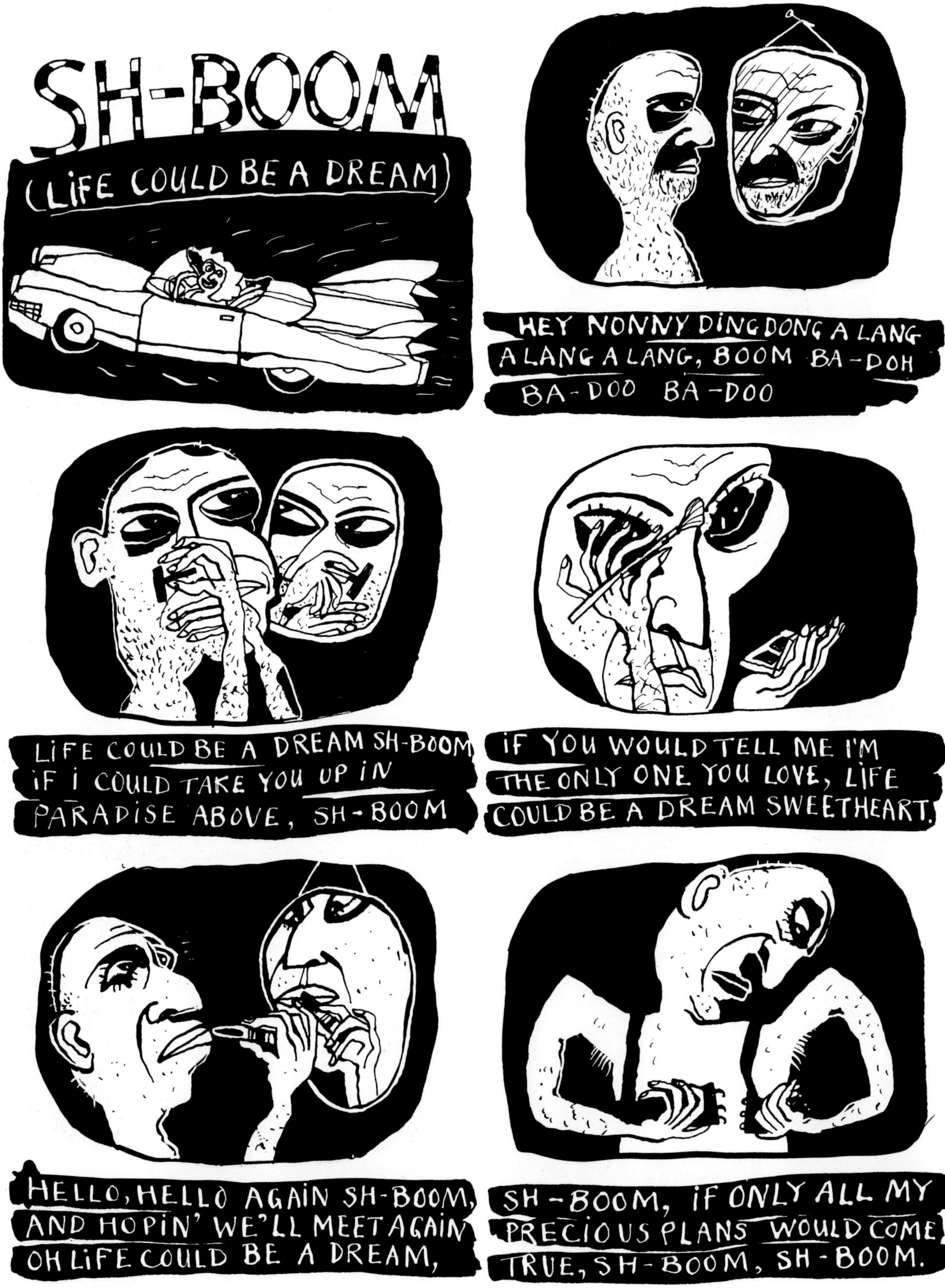
SH-BOOM
(LIFE COULD BE A DREAM)
HEY NONNY DING DONG A LANG A LANG A LANG, BOOM BA-DOH BA-DOO BA-DOO
LIFE COULD BE A DREAM SH-BOOM IF I COULD TAKE YOU UP IN PARADISE ABOVE, SH-BOOM
IF YOU WOULD TELL ME I'M THE ONLY ONE YOU LOVE, LIFE COULD BE A DREAM SWEETHEART.
HELLO, HELLO AGAIN SH-BOOM, AND HOPIN' WE'LL MEET AGAIN OH LIFE COULD BE A DREAM,
SH-BOOM, IF ONLY ALL MY PRECIOUS PLANS WOULD COME TRUE, SH-BOOM, SH-BOOM.

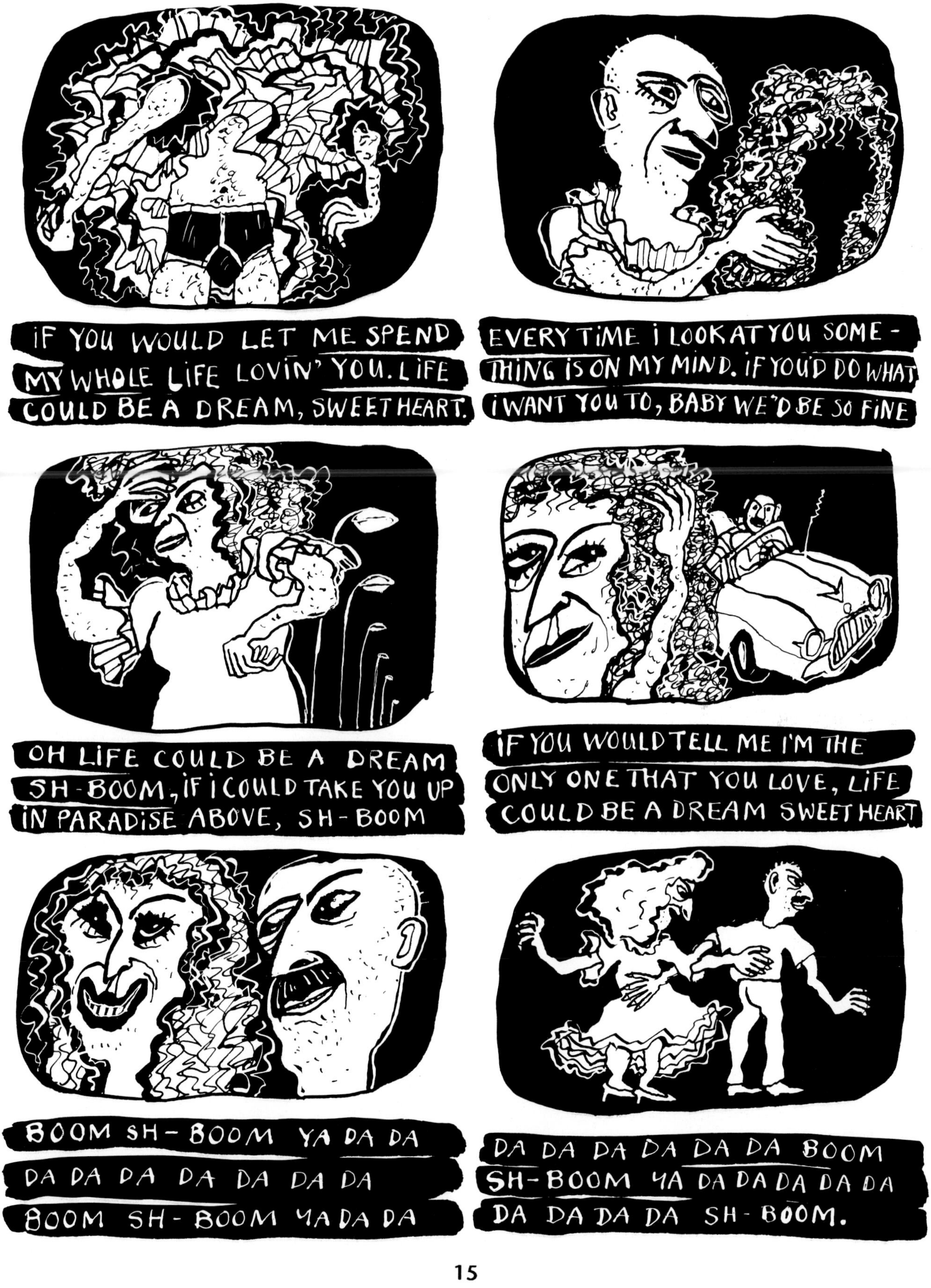
IF YOU WOULD LET ME SPEND MY WHOLE LIFE LOVIN' YOU. LIFE COULD BE A DREAM, SWEETHEART.
EVERY TIME I LOOK AT YOU SOME-THING IS ON MY MIND. IF YOU'D DO WHAT I WANT YOU TO, BABY WE'D BE SO FINE
OH LIFE COULD BE A DREAM SH-BOOM, IF I COULD TAKE YOU UP IN PARADISE ABOVE, SH-BOOM
IF YOU WOULD TELL ME I'M THE ONLY ONE THAT YOU LOVE, LIFE COULD BE A DREAM SWEETHEART
BOOM SH-BOOM YA DA DA DA DA DA DA DA DA DA BOOM SH-BOOM YA DA DA
DA DA DA DA DA DA BOOM SH-BOOM YA DA DA DA DA DA DA DA DA DA SH-BOOM.

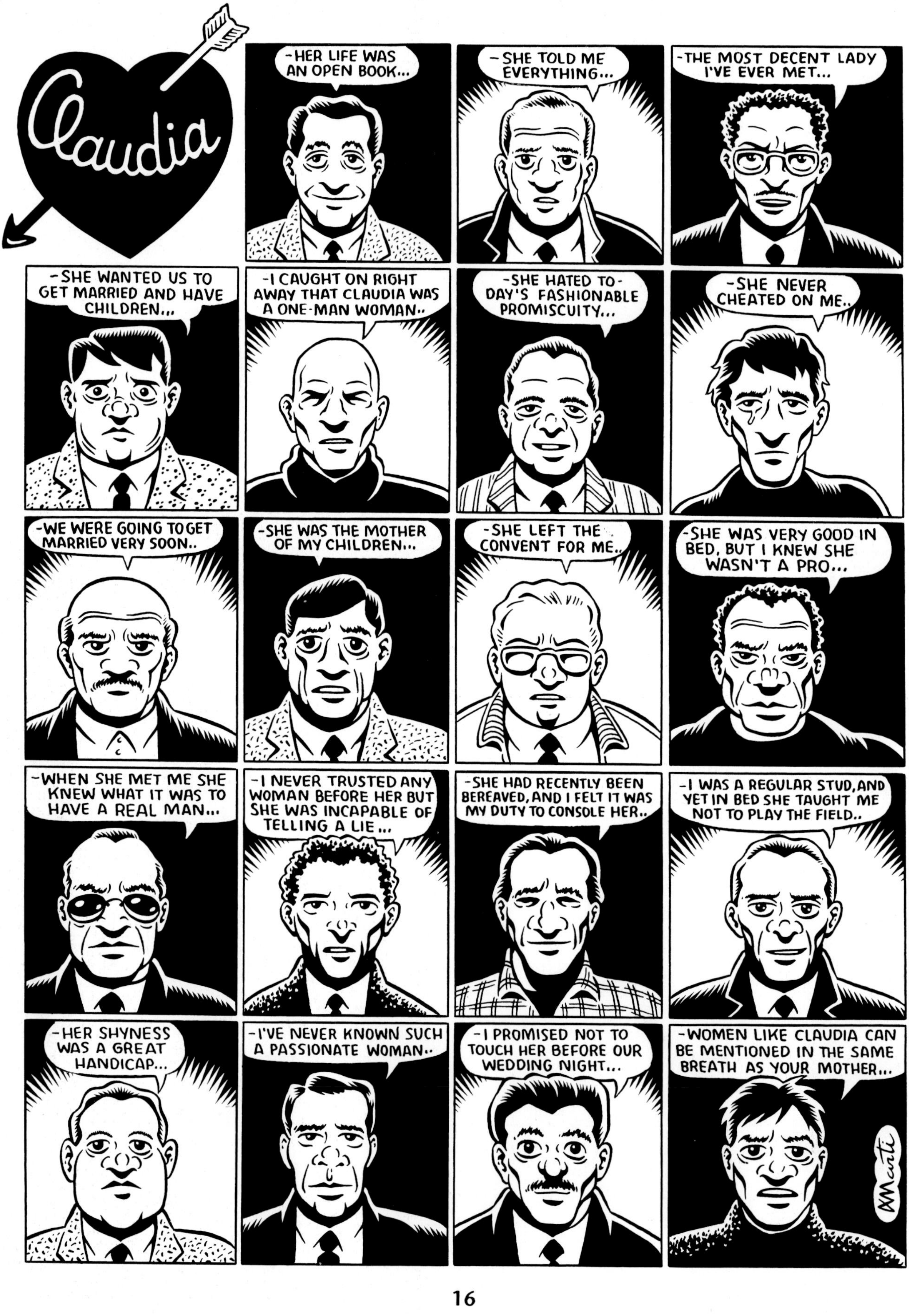
Claudia
-HER LIFE WAS AN OPEN BOOK...
-SHE TOLD ME EVERYTHING...
-THE MOST DECENT LADY I'VE EVER MET...
-SHE WANTED US TO GET MARRIED AND HAVE CHILDREN...
-I CAUGHT ON RIGHT AWAY THAT CLAUDIA WAS A ONE-MAN WOMAN..
-SHE HATED TO-DAY'S FASHIONABLE PROMISCUITY...
-SHE NEVER CHEATED ON ME..
-WE WERE GOING TO GET MARRIED VERY SOON..
-SHE WAS THE MOTHER OF MY CHILDREN...
-SHE LEFT THE CONVENT FOR ME..
-SHE WAS VERY GOOD IN BED, BUT I KNEW SHE WASN'T A PRO...
-WHEN SHE MET ME SHE KNEW WHAT IT WAS TO HAVE A REAL MAN...
-I NEVER TRUSTED ANY WOMAN BEFORE HER BUT SHE WAS INCAPABLE OF TELLING A LIE...
-SHE HAD RECENTLY BEEN BEREAVED, AND I FELT IT WAS MY DUTY TO CONSOLE HER..
-I WAS A REGULAR STUD, AND YET IN BED SHE TAUGHT ME NOT TO PLAY THE FIELD..
-HER SHYNESS WAS A GREAT HANDICAP...
-I'VE NEVER KNOWN SUCH A PASSIONATE WOMAN..
-I PROMISED NOT TO TOUCH HER BEFORE OUR WEDDING NIGHT...
-WOMEN LIKE CLAUDIA CAN BE MENTIONED IN THE SAME BREATH AS YOUR MOTHER...

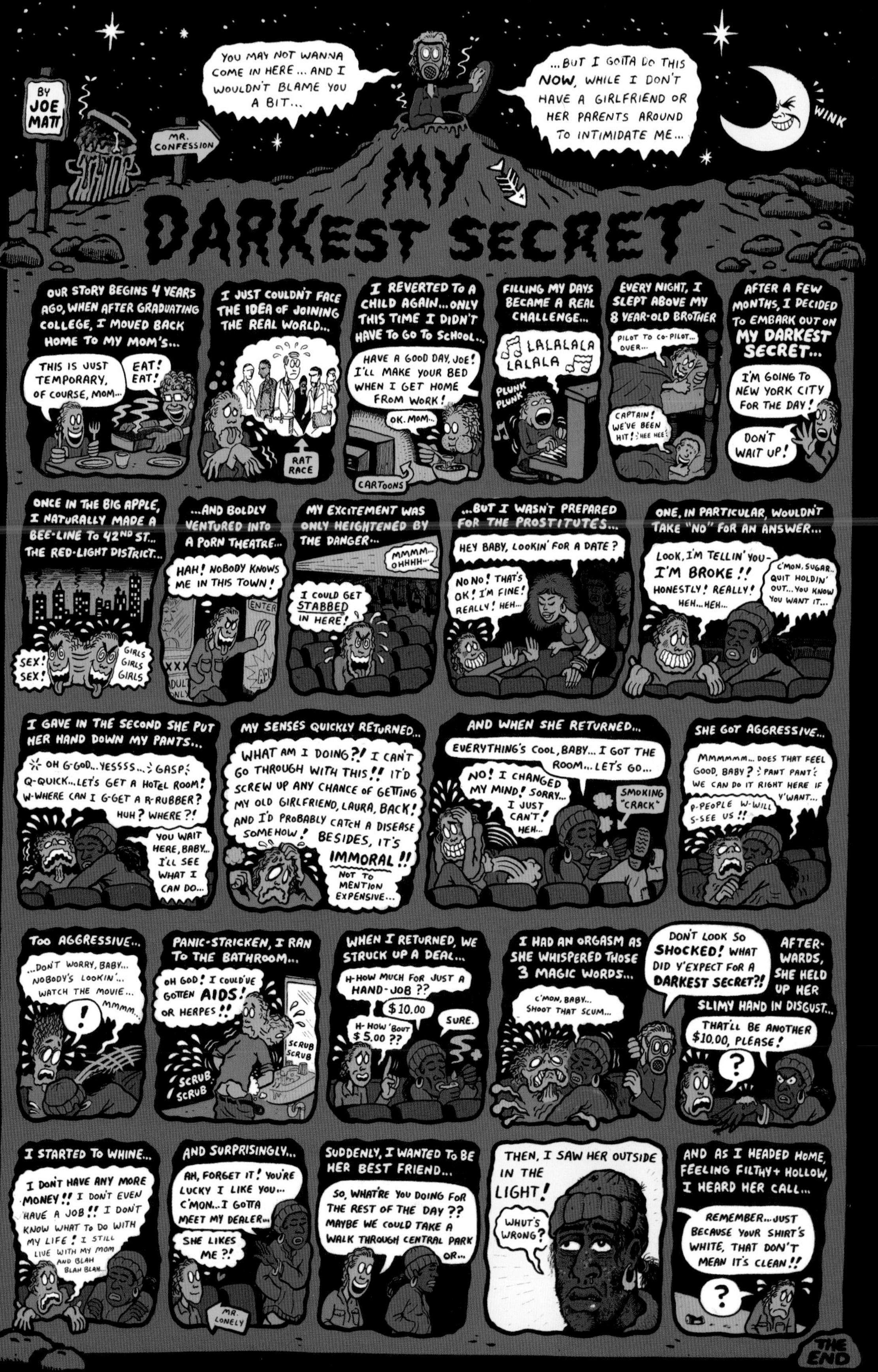

BY JOE MATT
MR. CONFESSION
YOU MAY NOT WANNA COME IN HERE... AND I WOULDN'T BLAME YOU A BIT...
...BUT I GOTTA DO THIS NOW, WHILE I DON'T HAVE A GIRLFRIEND OR HER PARENTS AROUND TO INTIMIDATE ME...
WINK
MY DARKEST SECRET
OUR STORY BEGINS 4 YEARS AGO, WHEN AFTER GRADUATING COLLEGE, I MOVED BACK HOME TO MY MOM'S...
THIS IS JUST TEMPORARY, OF COURSE, MOM...
EAT! EAT!
I JUST COULDN'T FACE THE IDEA OF JOINING THE REAL WORLD...
RAT RACE
I REVERTED TO A CHILD AGAIN... ONLY THIS TIME I DIDN'T HAVE TO GO TO SCHOOL...
HAVE A GOOD DAY, JOE! I'LL MAKE YOUR BED WHEN I GET HOME FROM WORK!
OK, MOM...
CARTOONS
FILLING MY DAYS BECAME A REAL CHALLENGE...
LALALALA LALALA
PLUNK PLUNK
EVERY NIGHT, I SLEPT ABOVE MY 8 YEAR-OLD BROTHER
PILOT TO CO-PILOT... OVER...
CAPTAIN! WE'VE BEEN HIT! HEE HEE
AFTER A FEW MONTHS, I DECIDED TO EMBARK OUT ON MY DARKEST SECRET...
I'M GOING TO NEW YORK CITY FOR THE DAY!
DON'T WAIT UP!
ONCE IN THE BIG APPLE, I NATURALLY MADE A BEE-LINE TO 42ND ST... THE RED-LIGHT DISTRICT...
SEX! SEX!
GIRLS GIRLS GIRLS
...AND BOLDLY VENTURED INTO A PORN THEATRE...
HAH! NOBODY KNOWS ME IN THIS TOWN!
ENTER
XXX
ADULTS ONLY
MY EXCITEMENT WAS ONLY HEIGHTENED BY THE DANGER...
MMMM... OHHHH...
I COULD GET STABBED IN HERE!
...BUT I WASN'T PREPARED FOR THE PROSTITUTES...
HEY BABY, LOOKIN' FOR A DATE?
NO NO! THAT'S OK! I'M FINE! REALLY! HEH...
ONE, IN PARTICULAR, WOULDN'T TAKE "NO" FOR AN ANSWER...
LOOK, I'M TELLIN' YOU- I'M BROKE!! HONESTLY! REALLY! HEH... HEH...
C'MON, SUGAR.. QUIT HOLDIN' OUT... YOU KNOW YOU WANT IT...
I GAVE IN THE SECOND SHE PUT HER HAND DOWN MY PANTS...
OH G-GOD... YESSSS... GASP Q-QUICK... LET'S GET A HOTEL ROOM! W-WHERE CAN I G-GET A R-RUBBER? HUH? WHERE?!
YOU WAIT HERE, BABY... I'LL SEE WHAT I CAN DO...
MY SENSES QUICKLY RETURNED...
WHAT AM I DOING?! I CAN'T GO THROUGH WITH THIS!! IT'D SCREW UP ANY CHANCE OF GETTING MY OLD GIRLFRIEND, LAURA, BACK! AND I'D PROBABLY CATCH A DISEASE SOMEHOW! BESIDES, IT'S IMMORAL!!
NOT TO MENTION EXPENSIVE...
AND WHEN SHE RETURNED...
EVERYTHING'S COOL, BABY... I GOT THE ROOM... LET'S GO...
NO! I CHANGED MY MIND! SORRY... I JUST CAN'T! HEH...
SMOKING "CRACK"
SHE GOT AGGRESSIVE...
MMMMMM... DOES THAT FEEL GOOD, BABY? PANT PANT WE CAN DO IT RIGHT HERE IF Y'WANT...
P-PEOPLE W-WILL S-SEE US!!
TOO AGGRESSIVE...
...DON'T WORRY, BABY... NOBODY'S LOOKIN'... WATCH THE MOVIE... MMMM...
!
PANIC-STRICKEN, I RAN TO THE BATHROOM...
OH GOD! I COULD'VE GOTTEN AIDS! OR HERPES!!
SCRUB SCRUB
SCRUB SCRUB
WHEN I RETURNED, WE STRUCK UP A DEAL...
H-HOW MUCH FOR JUST A HAND-JOB??
$10.00
H-HOW 'BOUT $5.00??
SURE.
I HAD AN ORGASM AS SHE WHISPERED THOSE 3 MAGIC WORDS...
C'MON, BABY... SHOOT THAT SCUM...
DON'T LOOK SO SHOCKED! WHAT DID Y'EXPECT FOR A DARKEST SECRET?!
AFTER-WARDS, SHE HELD UP HER SLIMY HAND IN DISGUST...
THAT'LL BE ANOTHER $10.00, PLEASE!
?
I STARTED TO WHINE...
I DON'T HAVE ANY MORE MONEY!! I DON'T EVEN HAVE A JOB!! I DON'T KNOW WHAT TO DO WITH MY LIFE! I STILL LIVE WITH MY MOM AND BLAH BLAH BLAH...
AND SURPRISINGLY...
AH, FORGET IT! YOU'RE LUCKY I LIKE YOU... C'MON.. I GOTTA MEET MY DEALER...
SHE LIKES ME?!
MR. LONELY
SUDDENLY, I WANTED TO BE HER BEST FRIEND...
SO, WHAT'RE YOU DOING FOR THE REST OF THE DAY?? MAYBE WE COULD TAKE A WALK THROUGH CENTRAL PARK OR...
THEN, I SAW HER OUTSIDE IN THE LIGHT!
WHUT'S WRONG?
AND AS I HEADED HOME, FEELING FILTHY + HOLLOW, I HEARD HER CALL...
REMEMBER... JUST BECAUSE YOUR SHIRT'S WHITE, THAT DON'T MEAN IT'S CLEAN!!
?
THE END

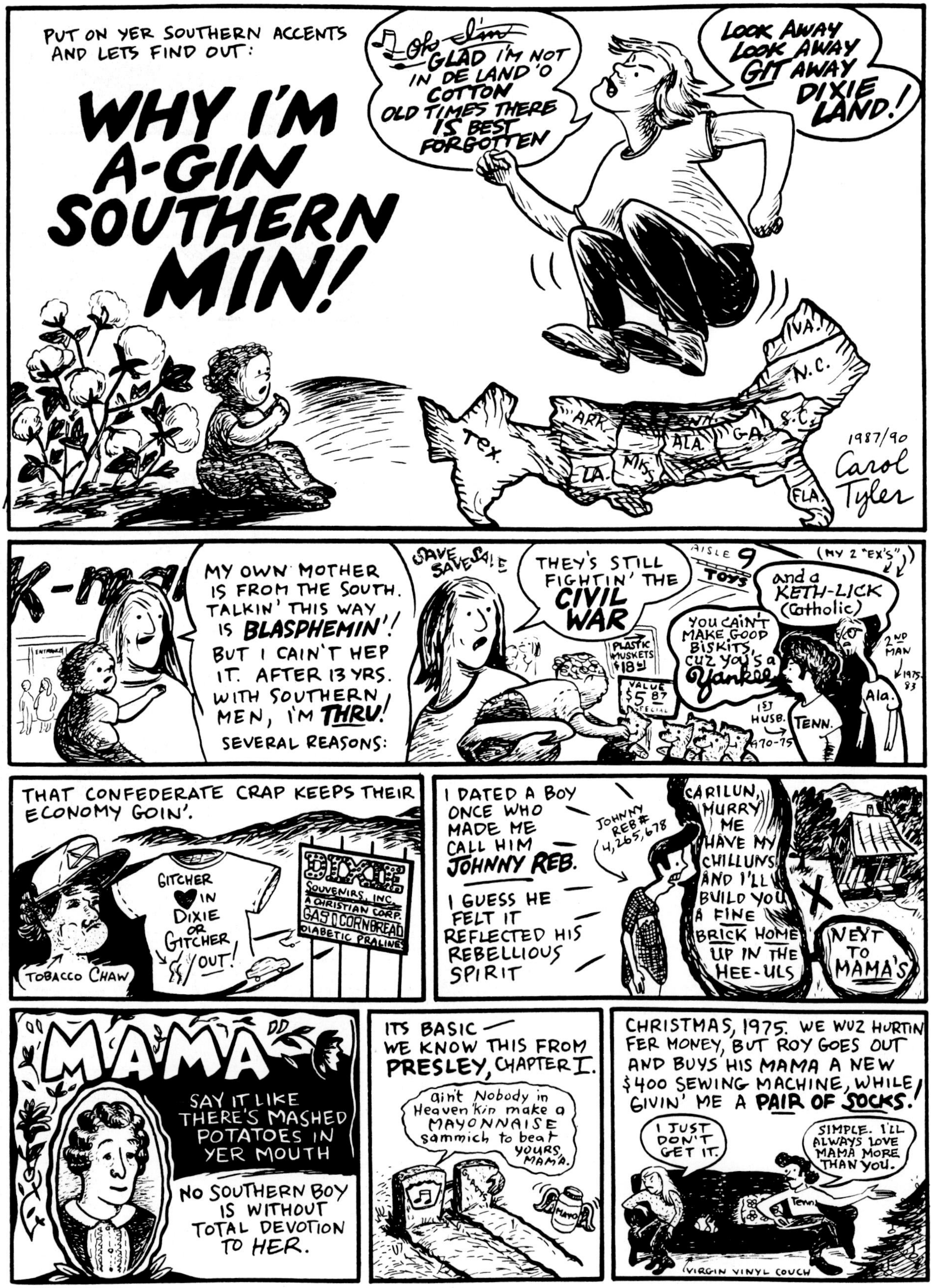
PUT ON YER SOUTHERN ACCENTS AND LETS FIND OUT:
WHY I'M A-GIN SOUTHERN MIN!
Oh I'm GLAD I'M NOT IN DE LAND 'O COTTON OLD TIMES THERE IS BEST FORGOTTEN
LOOK AWAY LOOK AWAY GIT AWAY DIXIE LAND!
VA.
N.C.
S.C.
GA.
ALA.
ARK.
MISS.
LA.
TEX.
FLA.
1987/90 Carol Tyler
K-mart
ENTRANCE
MY OWN MOTHER IS FROM THE SOUTH. TALKIN' THIS WAY IS BLASPHEMIN'! BUT I CAIN'T HEP IT. AFTER 13 YRS. WITH SOUTHERN MEN, I'M THRU! SEVERAL REASONS:
SAVE SAVE SALE
THEY'S STILL FIGHTIN' THE CIVIL WAR
AISLE 9 TOYS
PLASTIK MUSKETS $18
VALUE $5.87 SPECIAL
(MY 2 "EX'S")
and a KETH-LICK (Catholic)
YOU CAIN'T MAKE GOOD BISKITS, CUZ YOU'S A Yankee
2ND MAN 1975-83
Ala.
1ST HUSB. 1970-75
TENN.
THAT CONFEDERATE CRAP KEEPS THEIR ECONOMY GOIN'.
GITCHER ♥ IN DIXIE OR GITCHER OUT!
DIXIE SOUVENIRS, INC. A CHRISTIAN CORP.
GAS & CORNBREAD
DIABETIC PRALINES
TOBACCO CHAW
I DATED A BOY ONCE WHO MADE ME CALL HIM JOHNNY REB.
JOHNNY REB # 4,265,678
I GUESS HE FELT IT REFLECTED HIS REBELLIOUS SPIRIT
CARILUN, MURRY ME HAVE MY CHILLUNS AND I'LL BUILD YOU A FINE BRICK HOME UP IN THE HEE-ULS
NEXT TO MAMA'S
MAMA
SAY IT LIKE THERE'S MASHED POTATOES IN YER MOUTH
NO SOUTHERN BOY IS WITHOUT TOTAL DEVOTION TO HER.
ITS BASIC — WE KNOW THIS FROM PRESLEY, CHAPTER I.
ain't Nobody in Heaven kin make a MAYONNAISE sammich to beat YOURS, MAMA.
GLADYS
MAYO
CHRISTMAS, 1975. WE WUZ HURTIN FER MONEY, BUT ROY GOES OUT AND BUYS HIS MAMA A NEW $400 SEWING MACHINE, WHILE GIVIN' ME A PAIR OF SOCKS!
I JUST DON'T GET IT.
SIMPLE. I'LL ALWAYS LOVE MAMA MORE THAN YOU.
Tenn.
VIRGIN VINYL COUCH

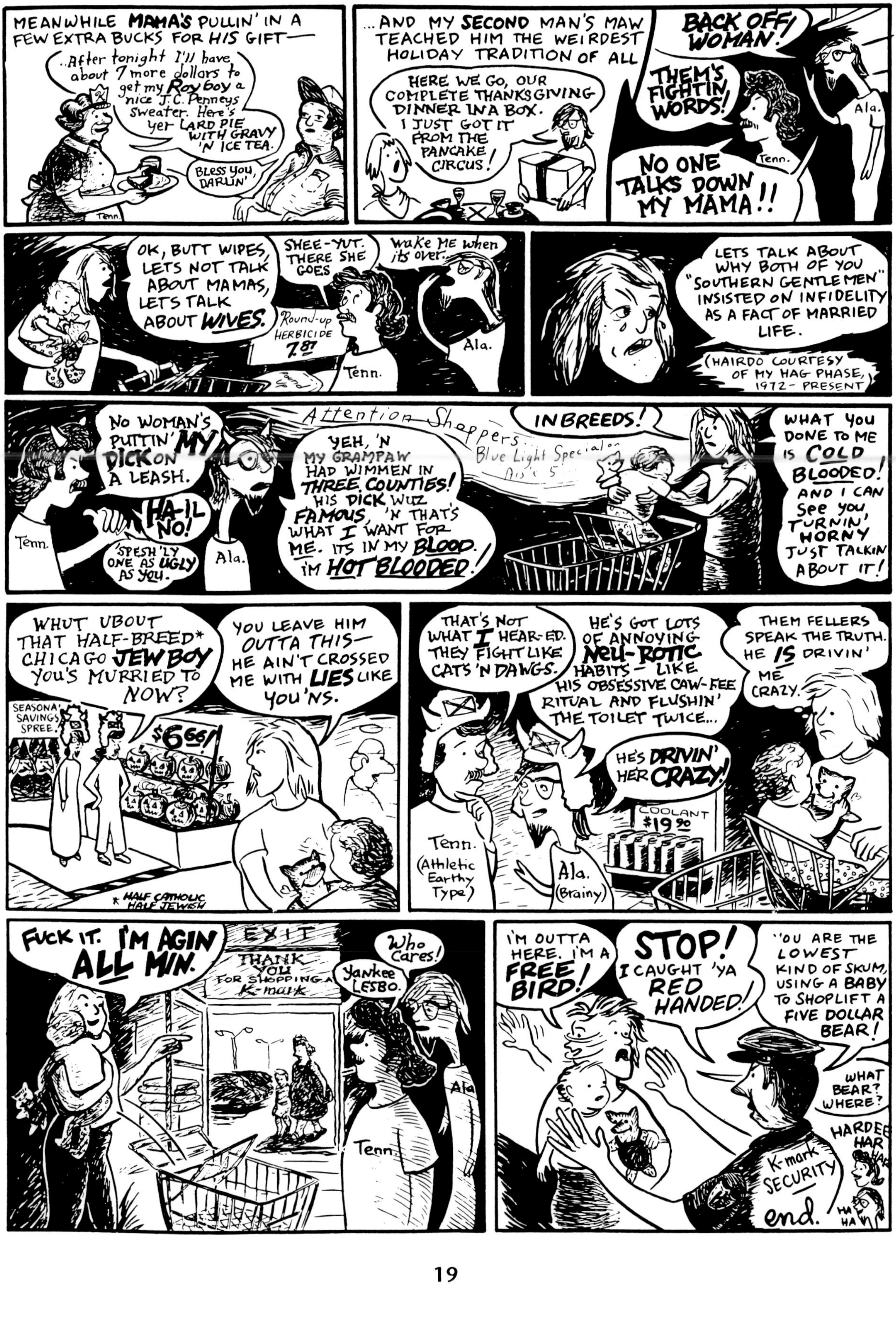
MEANWHILE MAMA'S PULLIN' IN A FEW EXTRA BUCKS FOR HIS GIFT—
..After tonight I'll have about 7 more dollars to get my Roy boy a nice J.C. Penneys sweater. Here's yer LARD PIE WITH GRAVY 'N ICE TEA.
BLESS YOU, DARLIN'
Tenn.
...AND MY SECOND MAN'S MAW TEACHED HIM THE WEIRDEST HOLIDAY TRADITION OF ALL
HERE WE GO, OUR COMPLETE THANKSGIVING DINNER IN A BOX. I JUST GOT IT FROM THE PANCAKE CIRCUS!
BACK OFF, WOMAN!
THEM'S FIGHTIN WORDS!
Ala.
Tenn.
NO ONE TALKS DOWN MY MAMA!!
OK, BUTT WIPES, LETS NOT TALK ABOUT MAMAS, LETS TALK ABOUT WIVES.
SHEE-YUT. THERE SHE GOES
Wake me when its over.
Round-up HERBICIDE 7.87
Ala.
Tenn.
LETS TALK ABOUT WHY BOTH OF YOU "SOUTHERN GENTLEMEN" INSISTED ON INFIDELITY AS A FACT OF MARRIED LIFE.
(HAIRDO COURTESY OF MY HAG PHASE, 1972-PRESENT)
NO WOMAN'S PUTTIN' MY DICK ON A LEASH.
HA-IL NO!
'SPESH'LY ONE AS UGLY AS YOU.
Tenn.
Ala.
Attention Shoppers
Blue Light Special on
YEH, 'N MY GRAMPAW HAD WIMMEN IN THREE COUNTIES! HIS DICK WUZ FAMOUS, 'N THAT'S WHAT I WANT FOR ME. ITS IN MY BLOOD. I'M HOT BLOODED!
INBREEDS!
WHAT YOU DONE TO ME IS COLD BLOODED! AND I CAN SEE YOU, TURNIN' HORNY JUST TALKIN ABOUT IT!
WHUT UBOUT THAT HALF-BREED* CHICAGO JEW BOY YOU'S MURRIED TO NOW?
YOU LEAVE HIM OUTTA THIS— HE AIN'T CROSSED ME WITH LIES LIKE YOU'NS.
SEASONAL SAVINGS SPREE
$6.66!
* HALF CATHOLIC HALF JEWISH
THAT'S NOT WHAT I HEAR-ED. THEY FIGHT LIKE CATS 'N DAWGS.
HE'S GOT LOTS OF ANNOYING NEU-ROTIC HABITS – LIKE HIS OBSESSIVE CAW-FEE RITUAL AND FLUSHIN' THE TOILET TWICE...
THEM FELLERS SPEAK THE TRUTH. HE IS DRIVIN' ME CRAZY.
HE'S DRIVIN' HER CRAZY!
COOLANT $19.90
Tenn. (Athletic Earthy Type)
Ala. (Brainy)
FUCK IT. I'M AGIN ALL MIN.
EXIT
THANK YOU FOR SHOPPING AT K-mark
Who cares!
Yankee LESBO.
Ala
Tenn.
I'M OUTTA HERE. I'M A FREE BIRD!
STOP! I CAUGHT 'YA RED HANDED!
"OU ARE THE LOWEST KIND OF SKUM, USING A BABY TO SHOPLIFT A FIVE DOLLAR BEAR!
WHAT BEAR? WHERE?
HARDEE HAR HAR
K-mark SECURITY
HA HA
end.

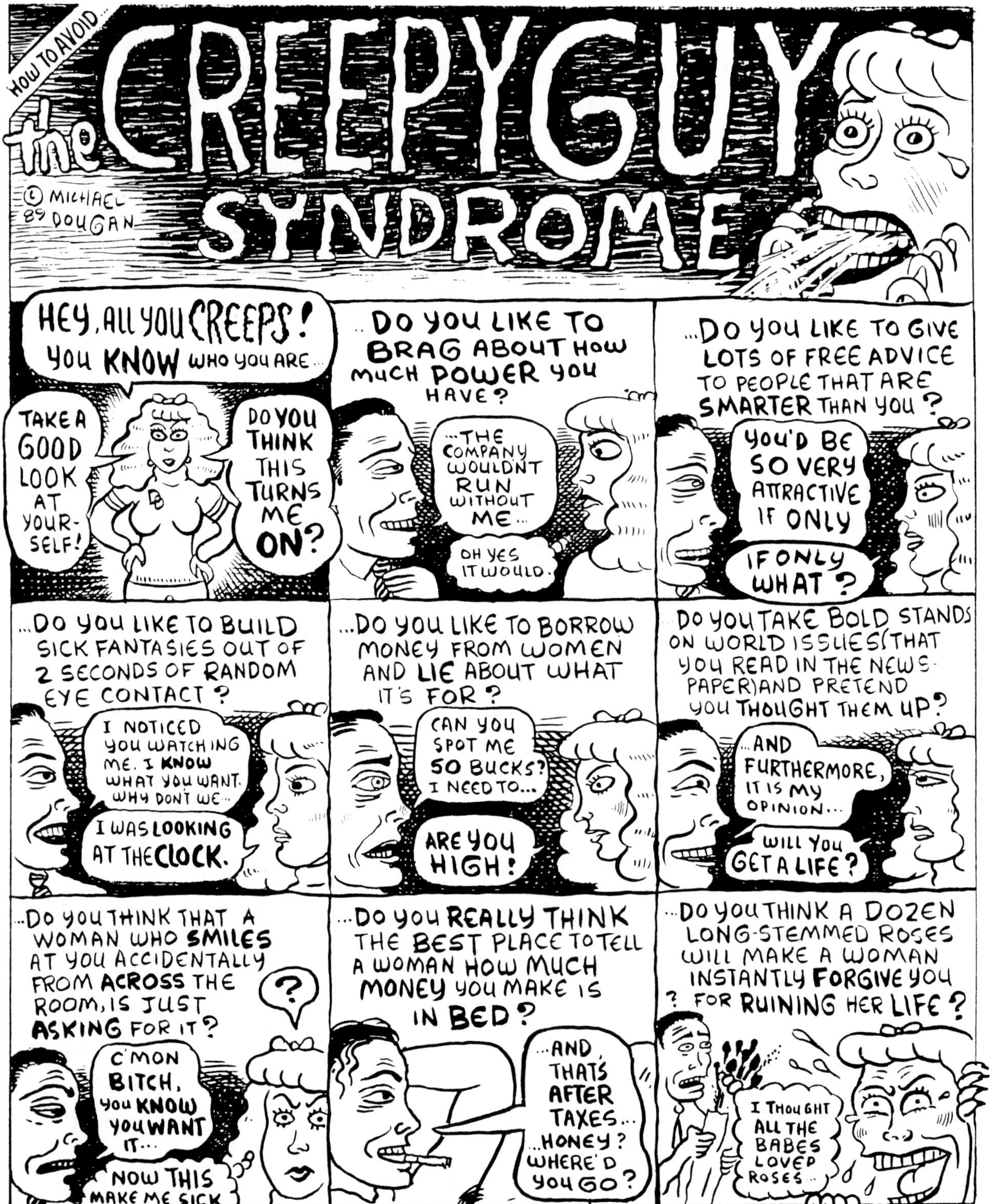
HOW TO AVOID...
the CREEPY GUY SYNDROME
© MICHAEL 89 DOUGAN
HEY, ALL YOU CREEPS! YOU KNOW WHO YOU ARE...
TAKE A GOOD LOOK AT YOURSELF!
DO YOU THINK THIS TURNS ME ON?
...DO YOU LIKE TO BRAG ABOUT HOW MUCH POWER YOU HAVE?
...THE COMPANY WOULDN'T RUN WITHOUT ME...
OH YES IT WOULD.
...DO YOU LIKE TO GIVE LOTS OF FREE ADVICE TO PEOPLE THAT ARE SMARTER THAN YOU?
YOU'D BE SO VERY ATTRACTIVE IF ONLY
IF ONLY WHAT?
...DO YOU LIKE TO BUILD SICK FANTASIES OUT OF 2 SECONDS OF RANDOM EYE CONTACT?
I NOTICED YOU WATCHING ME. I KNOW WHAT YOU WANT. WHY DON'T WE...
I WAS LOOKING AT THE CLOCK.
...DO YOU LIKE TO BORROW MONEY FROM WOMEN AND LIE ABOUT WHAT IT'S FOR?
CAN YOU SPOT ME 50 BUCKS? I NEED TO...
ARE YOU HIGH!
...DO YOU TAKE BOLD STANDS ON WORLD ISSUES (THAT YOU READ IN THE NEWSPAPER) AND PRETEND YOU THOUGHT THEM UP?
...AND FURTHERMORE, IT IS MY OPINION...
WILL YOU GET A LIFE?
...DO YOU THINK THAT A WOMAN WHO SMILES AT YOU ACCIDENTALLY FROM ACROSS THE ROOM, IS JUST ASKING FOR IT?
?
C'MON BITCH, YOU KNOW YOU WANT IT...
NOW THIS MAKE ME SICK
...DO YOU REALLY THINK THE BEST PLACE TO TELL A WOMAN HOW MUCH MONEY YOU MAKE IS IN BED?
...AND, THAT'S AFTER TAXES... ...HONEY? WHERE'D YOU GO?
...DO YOU THINK A DOZEN LONG-STEMMED ROSES WILL MAKE A WOMAN INSTANTLY FORGIVE YOU FOR RUINING HER LIFE?
?
I THOUGHT ALL THE BABES LOVED ROSES...

TALKIN' NINETIES

ROBERTA GREGORY

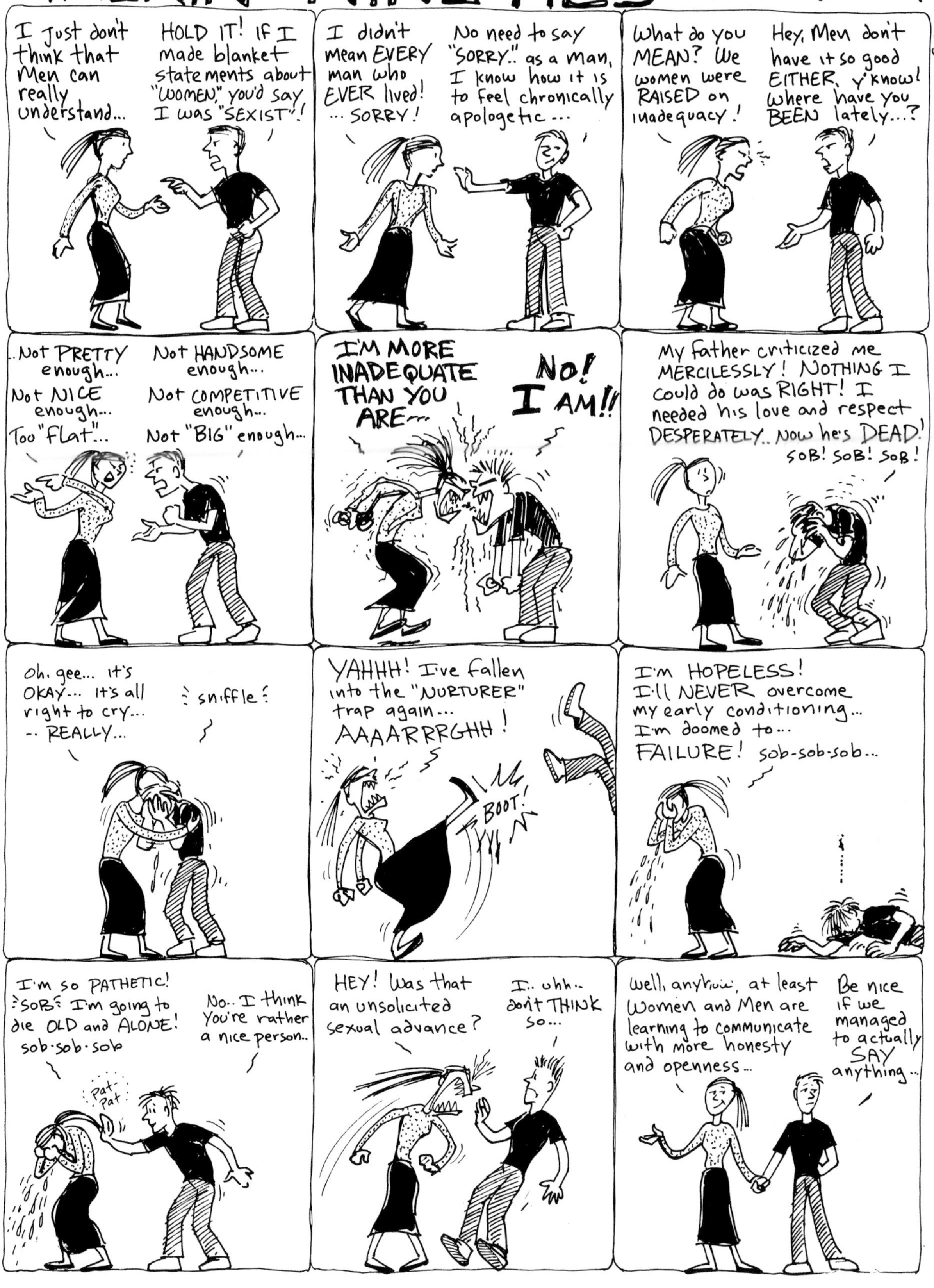
©91
I just don't think that Men can really understand...
HOLD IT! IF I made blanket statements about "WOMEN," you'd say I was "SEXIST"!
I didn't mean EVERY man who EVER lived! ... SORRY!
No need to say "SORRY".. as a man, I know how it is to feel chronically apologetic...
What do you MEAN? We women were RAISED on inadequacy!
Hey, Men don't have it so good EITHER, y'know! Where have you BEEN lately...?
..Not PRETTY enough...
Not HANDSOME enough...
Not NICE enough...
Not COMPETITIVE enough...
Too "Flat"...
Not "BIG" enough...
I'M MORE INADEQUATE THAN YOU ARE--
NO! I AM!!
My father criticized me MERCILESSLY! NOTHING I could do was RIGHT! I needed his love and respect DESPERATELY.. Now he's DEAD!
SOB! SOB! SOB!
oh, gee... it's OKAY... it's all right to cry... -- REALLY...
sniffle
YAHHH! I've fallen into the "NURTURER" trap again... AAAARRRGHH!
BOOT!
I'M HOPELESS! I'LL NEVER overcome my early conditioning... I'm doomed to... FAILURE! sob-sob-sob...
I'm so PATHETIC! SOB I'm going to die OLD and ALONE! sob-sob-sob
No.. I think you're rather a nice person..
Pat-Pat
HEY! Was that an unsolicited sexual advance?
I.. uhh.. don't THINK so...
Well, anyhow, at least Women and Men are learning to communicate with more honesty and openness...
Be nice if we managed to actually SAY anything...

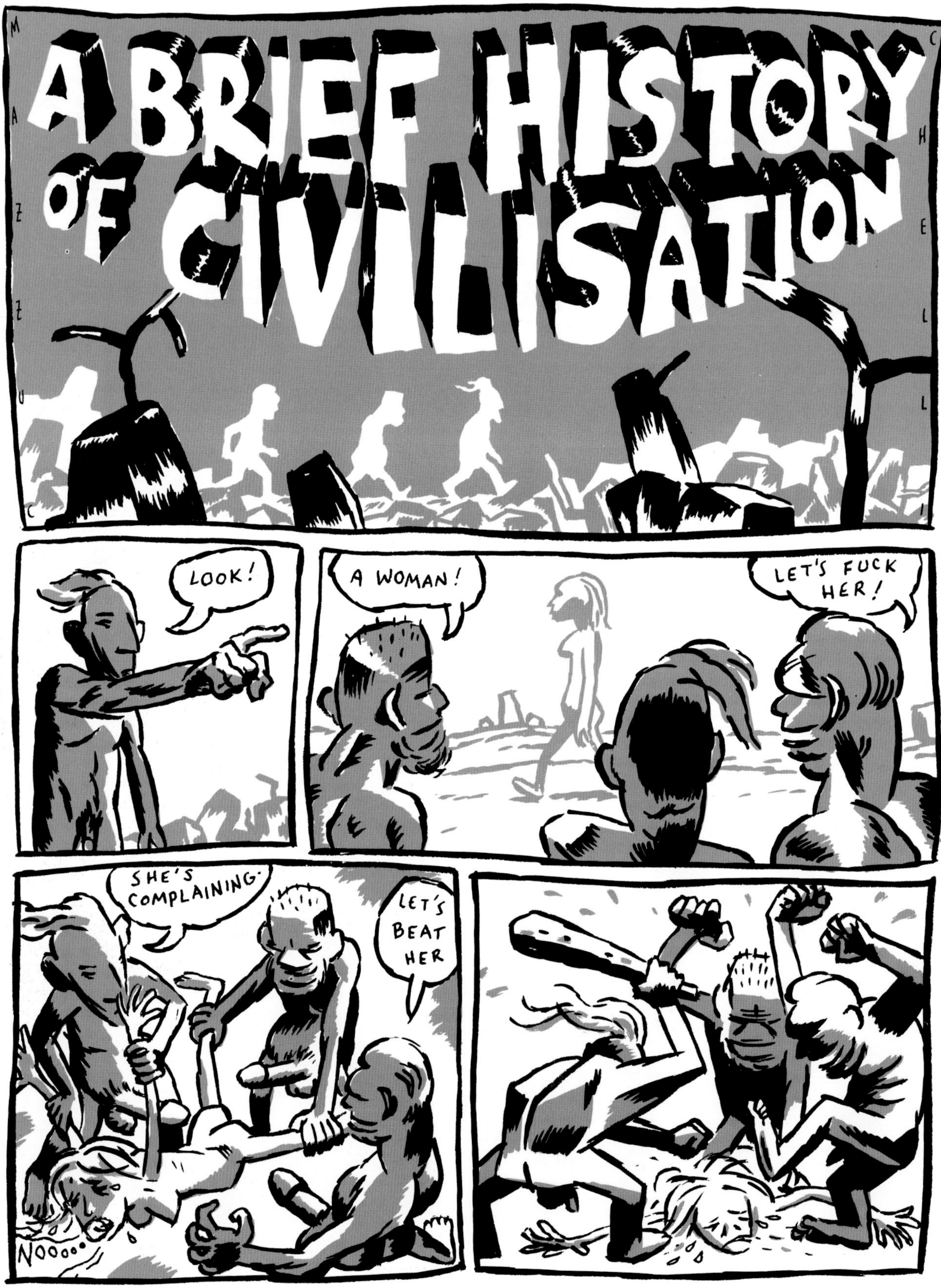
MAZZUC
CHELLI
A BRIEF HISTORY OF CIVILISATION
LOOK!
A WOMAN!
LET'S FUCK HER!
SHE'S COMPLAINING.
LET'S BEAT HER
NOoooo

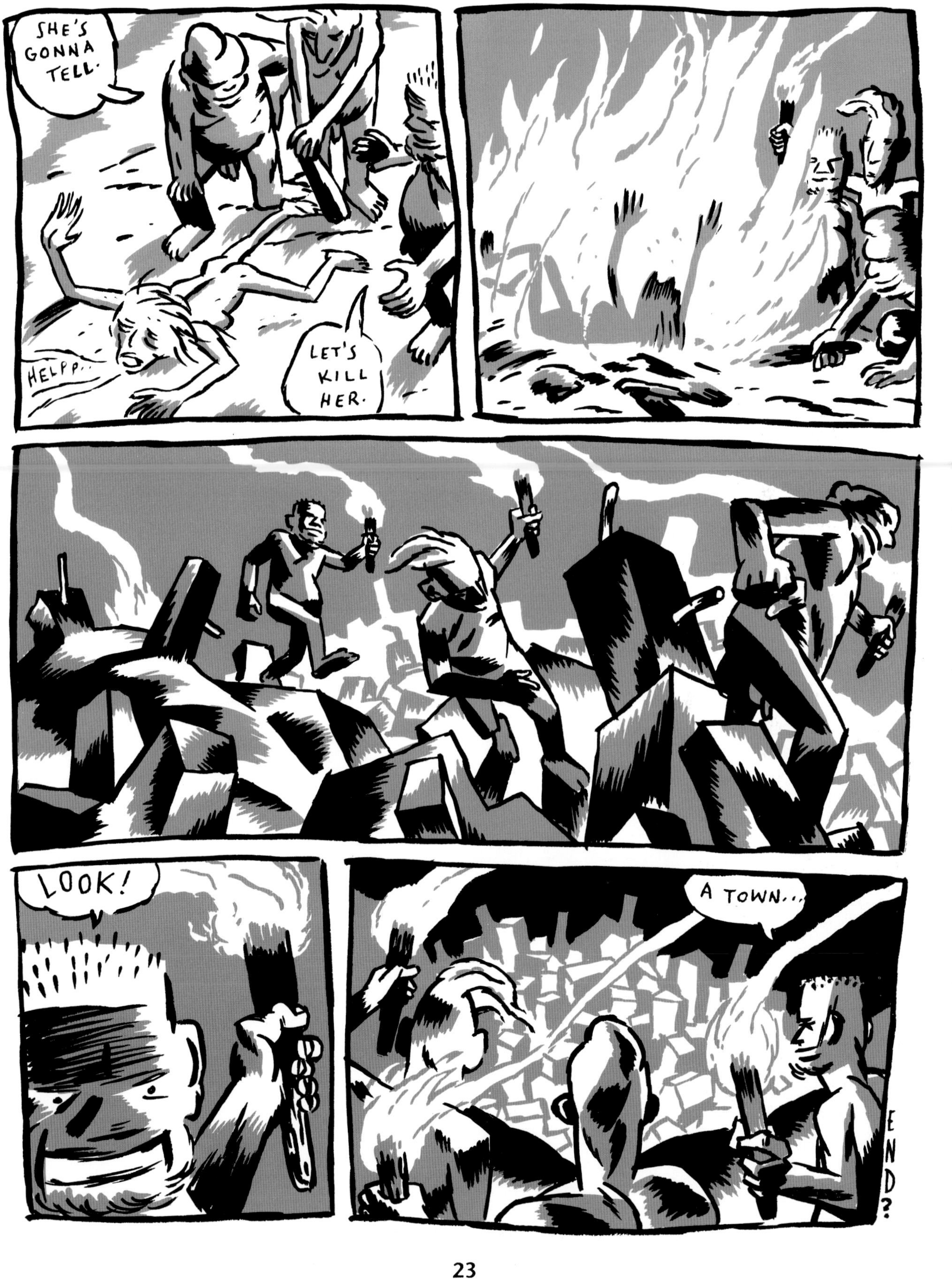
SHE'S GONNA TELL.
HELPP..
LET'S KILL HER.
LOOK!
A TOWN...
END?

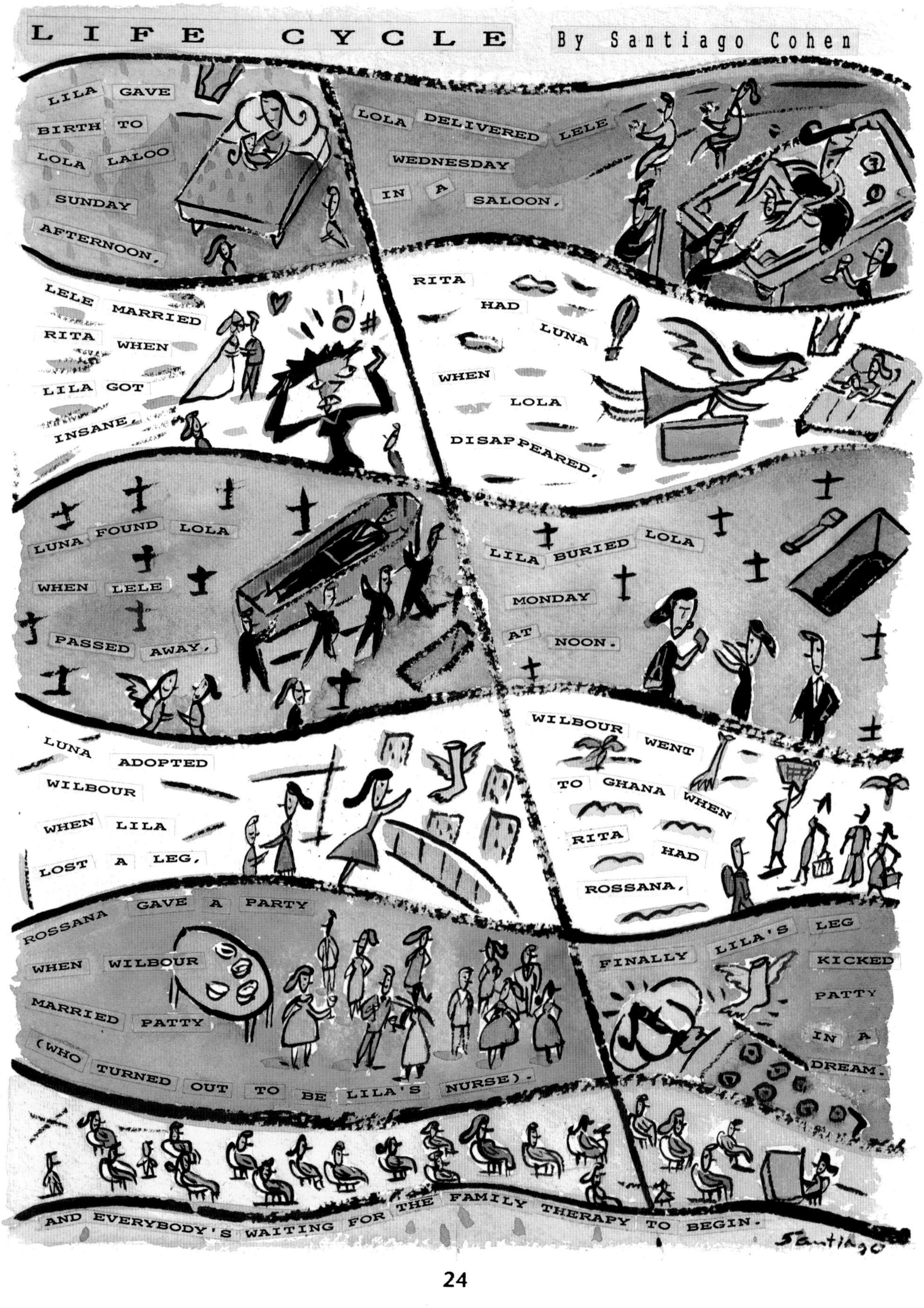
LIFE CYCLE
By Santiago Cohen
LILA GAVE BIRTH TO LOLA LALOO SUNDAY AFTERNOON,
LOLA DELIVERED LELE WEDNESDAY IN A SALOON,
LELE MARRIED RITA WHEN LILA GOT INSANE,
RITA HAD LUNA WHEN LOLA DISAPPEARED.
LUNA FOUND LOLA WHEN LELE PASSED AWAY,
LILA BURIED LOLA MONDAY AT NOON.
LUNA ADOPTED WILBOUR WHEN LILA LOST A LEG,
WILBOUR WENT TO GHANA WHEN RITA HAD ROSSANA,
ROSSANA GAVE A PARTY WHEN WILBOUR MARRIED PATTY (WHO TURNED OUT TO BE LILA'S NURSE).
FINALLY LILA'S LEG KICKED PATTY IN A DREAM.
AND EVERYBODY'S WAITING FOR THE FAMILY THERAPY TO BEGIN.
Santiago

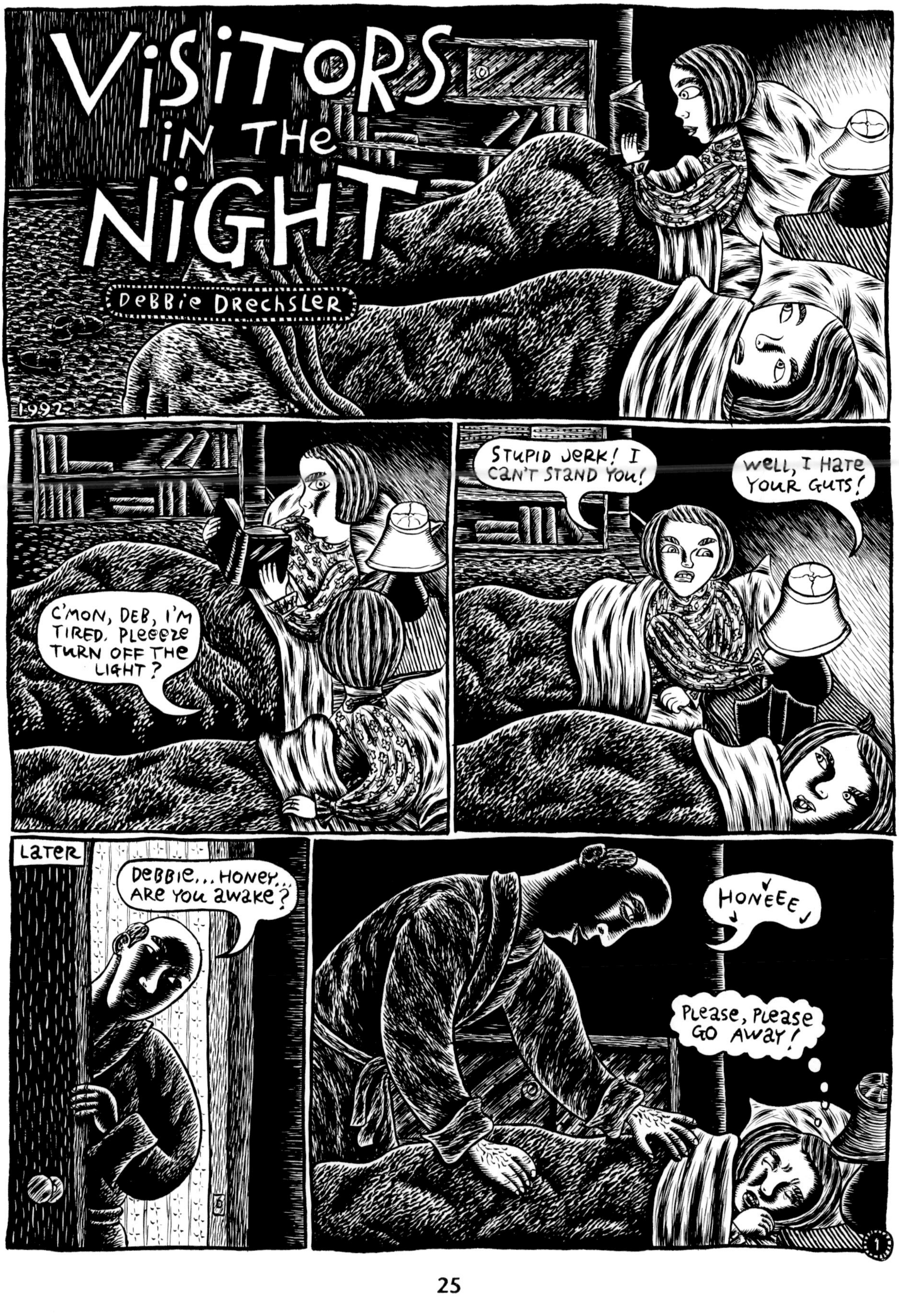
Visitors in the Night
Debbie Drechsler
1992
C'MON, DEB, I'M TIRED. PLEEEZE TURN OFF THE LIGHT?
STUPID JERK! I CAN'T STAND YOU!
WELL, I HATE YOUR GUTS!
LATER
DEBBIE... HONEY, ARE YOU AWAKE?
HONEEE
PLEASE, PLEASE GO AWAY!
1

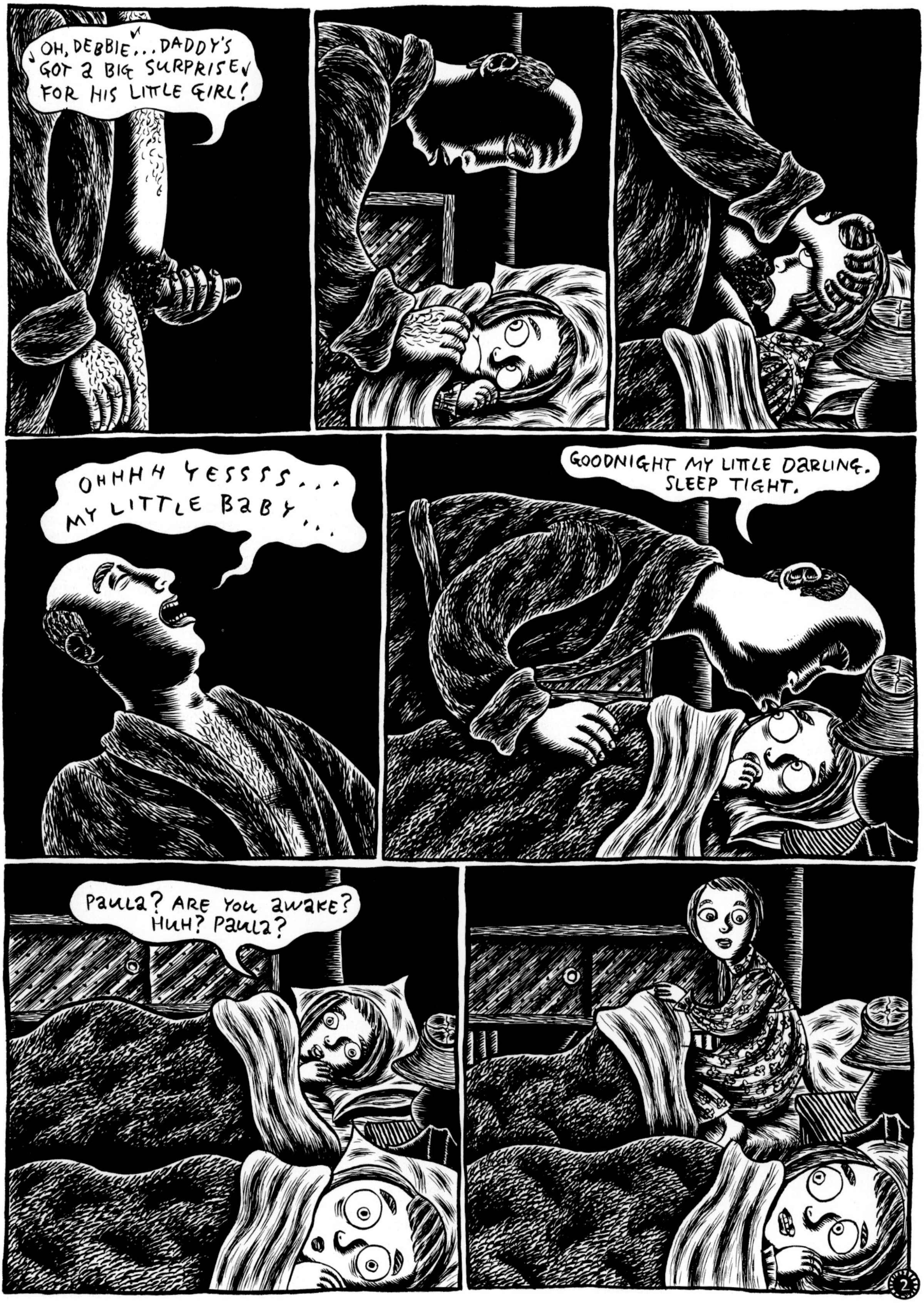
OH, DEBBIE... DADDY'S GOT A BIG SURPRISE FOR HIS LITTLE GIRL!
OHHHH YESSSS... MY LITTLE BABY...
GOODNIGHT MY LITTLE DARLING. SLEEP TIGHT.
PAULA? ARE YOU AWAKE? HUH? PAULA?

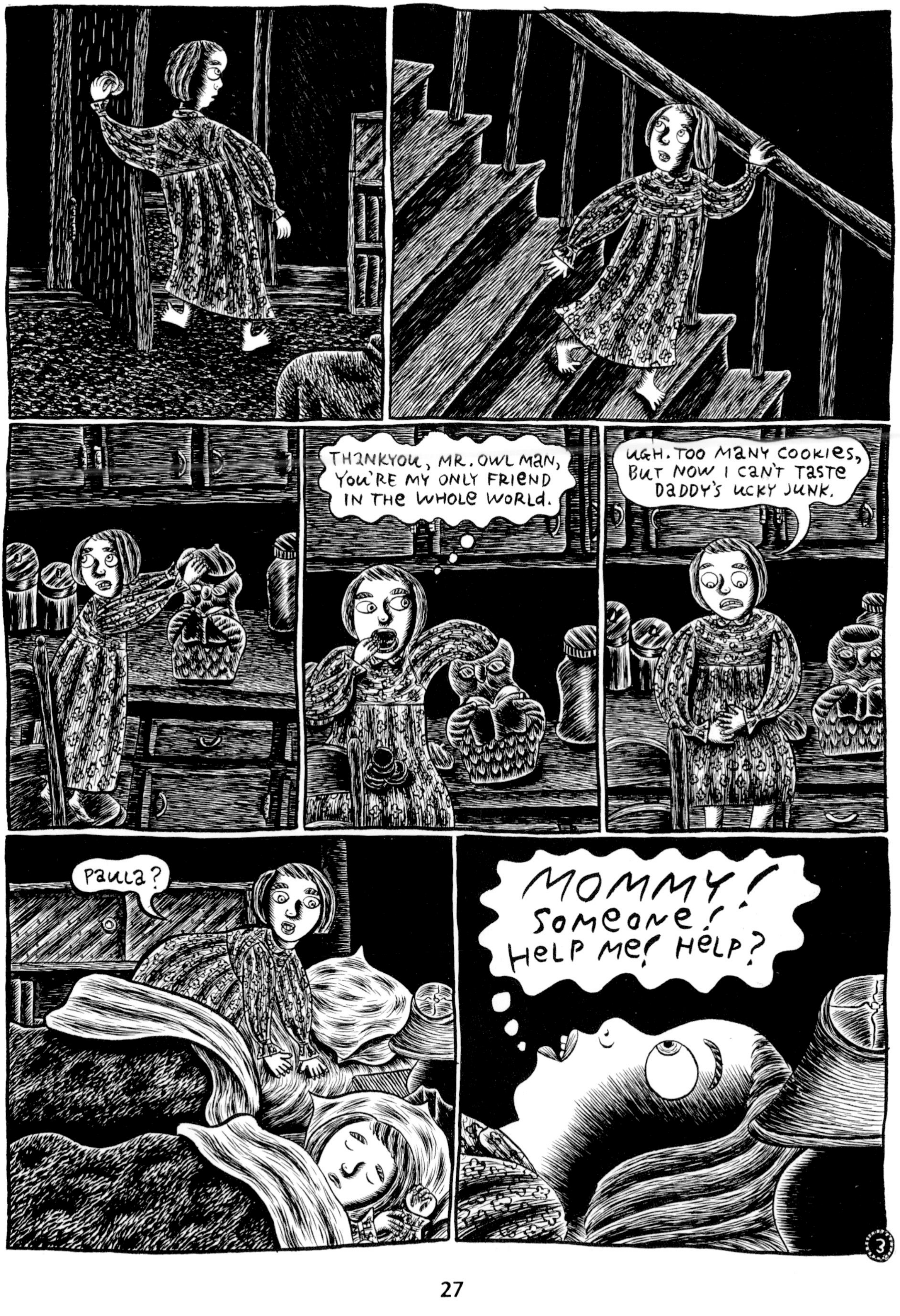
THANKYOU, MR. OWL MAN, YOU'RE MY ONLY FRIEND IN THE WHOLE WORLD.
UGH. TOO MANY COOKIES, BUT NOW I CAN'T TASTE DADDY'S UCKY JUNK.
PAULA?
MOMMY! SOMEONE! HELP ME! HELP?
3

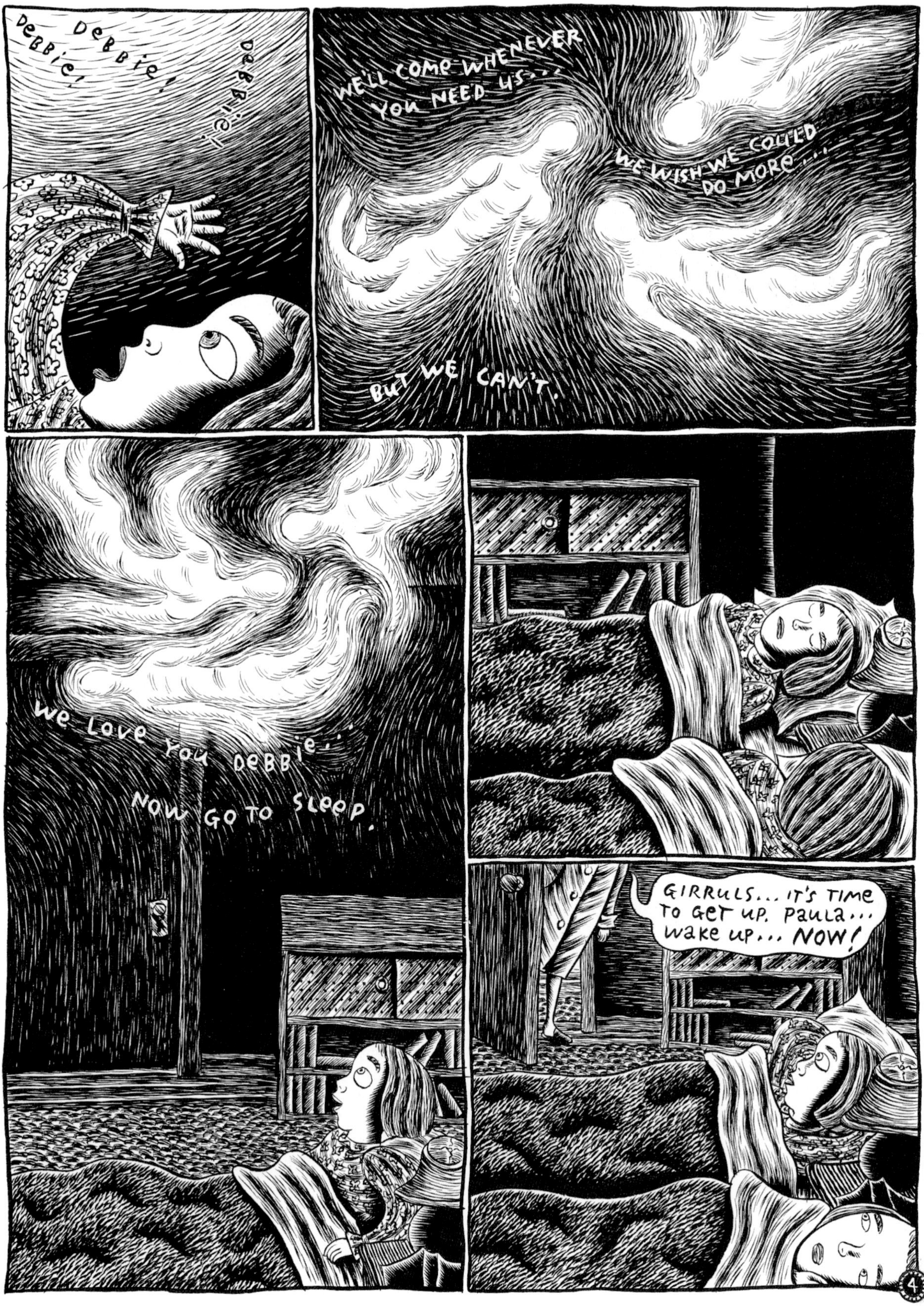
DEBBIE! DEBBIE! DEBBIE!
WE'LL COME WHENEVER YOU NEED US...
WE WISH WE COULD DO MORE...
BUT WE CAN'T.
WE LOVE YOU DEBBIE...
NOW GO TO SLEEP.
GIRRULS... IT'S TIME TO GET UP. PAULA... WAKE UP... NOW!

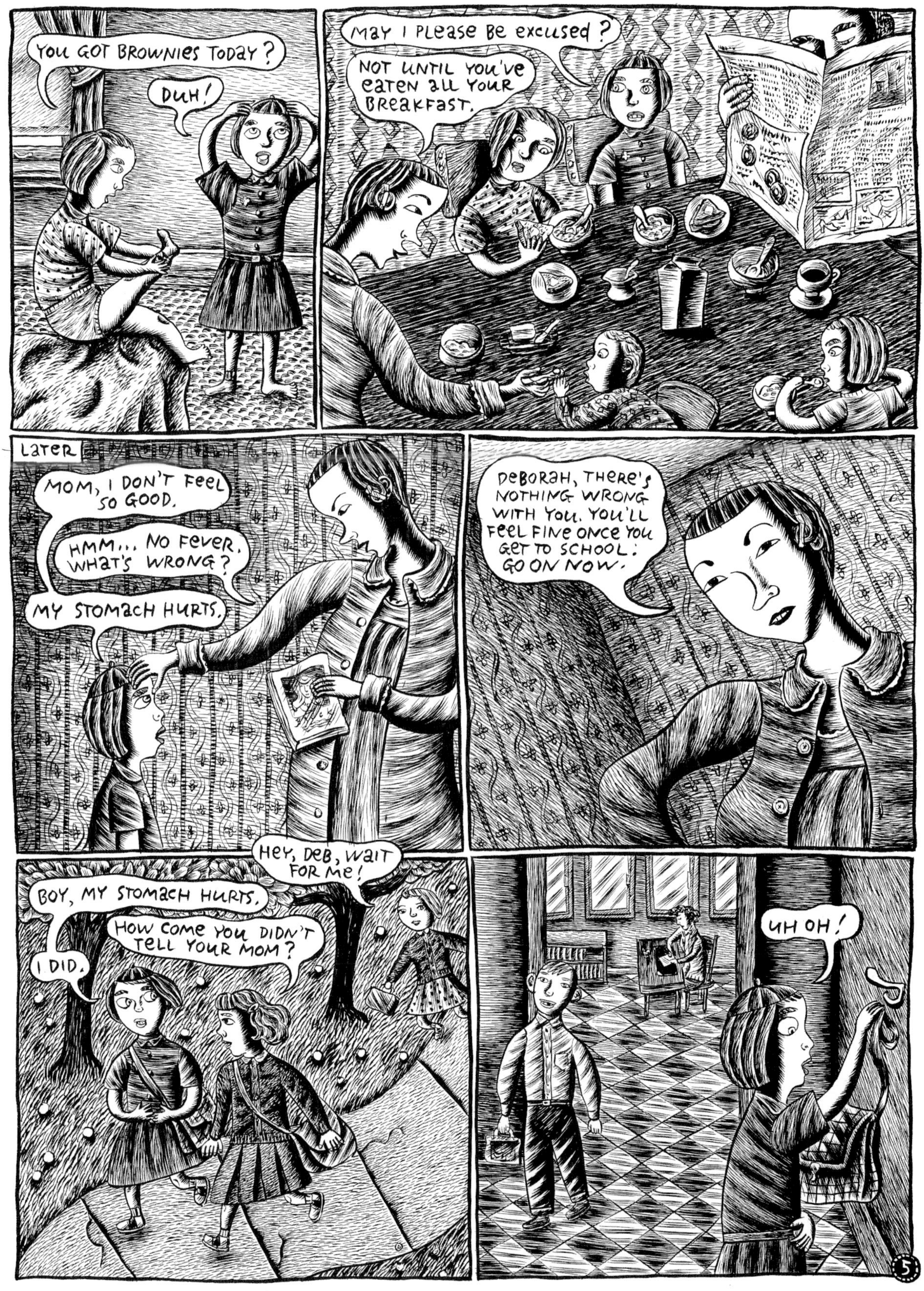
YOU GOT BROWNIES TODAY?
DUH!
MAY I PLEASE BE EXCUSED?
NOT UNTIL YOU'VE EATEN ALL YOUR BREAKFAST.
LATER
MOM, I DON'T FEEL SO GOOD.
HMM... NO FEVER. WHAT'S WRONG?
MY STOMACH HURTS.
DEBORAH, THERE'S NOTHING WRONG WITH YOU. YOU'LL FEEL FINE ONCE YOU GET TO SCHOOL. GO ON NOW.
BOY, MY STOMACH HURTS.
HEY, DEB, WAIT FOR ME!
HOW COME YOU DIDN'T TELL YOUR MOM?
I DID.
UH OH!
5

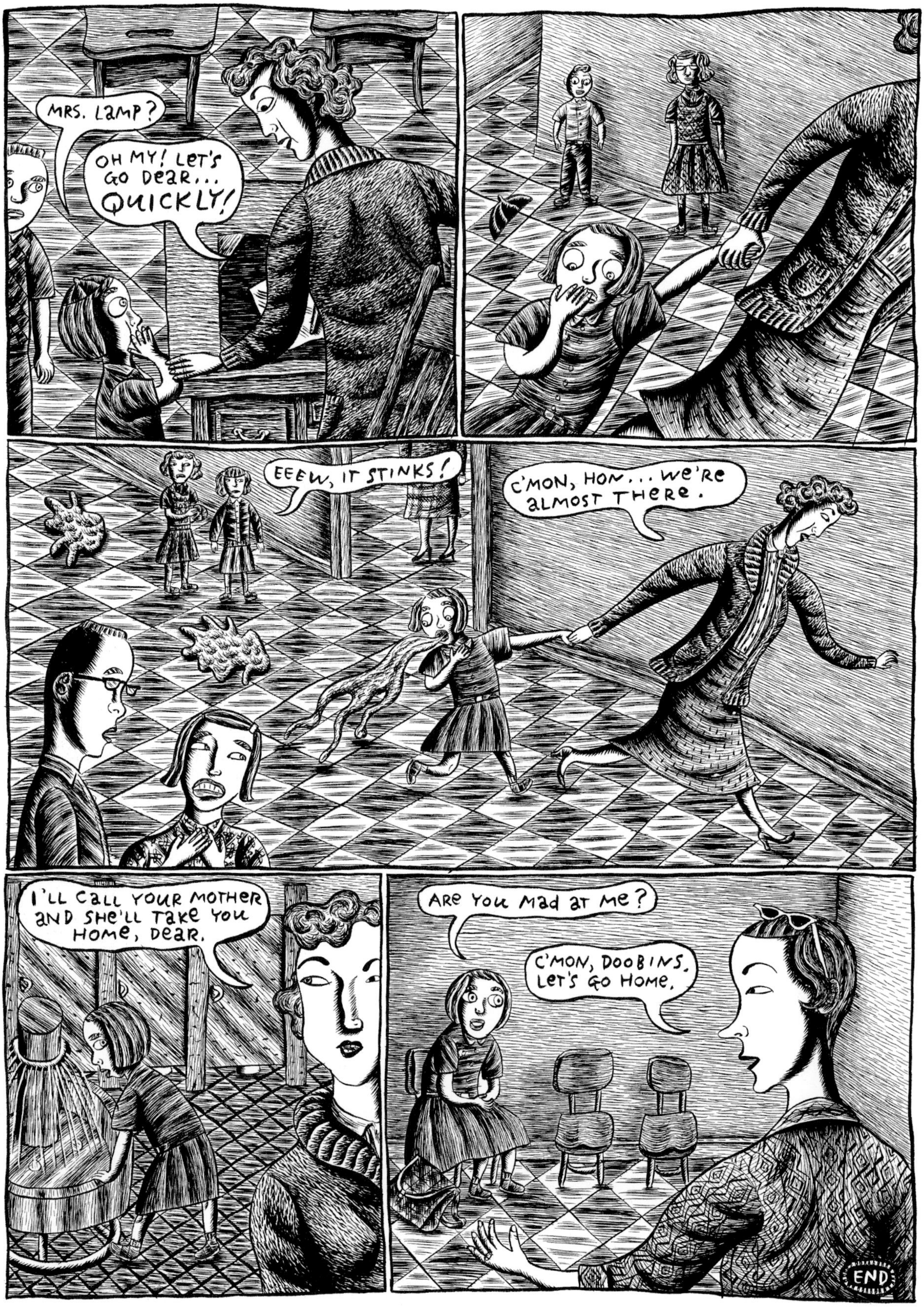
MRS. LAMP?
OH MY! LET'S GO DEAR... QUICKLY!
EEEW, IT STINKS!
C'MON, HON... WE'RE ALMOST THERE.
I'LL CALL YOUR MOTHER AND SHE'LL TAKE YOU HOME, DEAR.
ARE YOU MAD AT ME?
C'MON, DOOBINS. LET'S GO HOME.
END

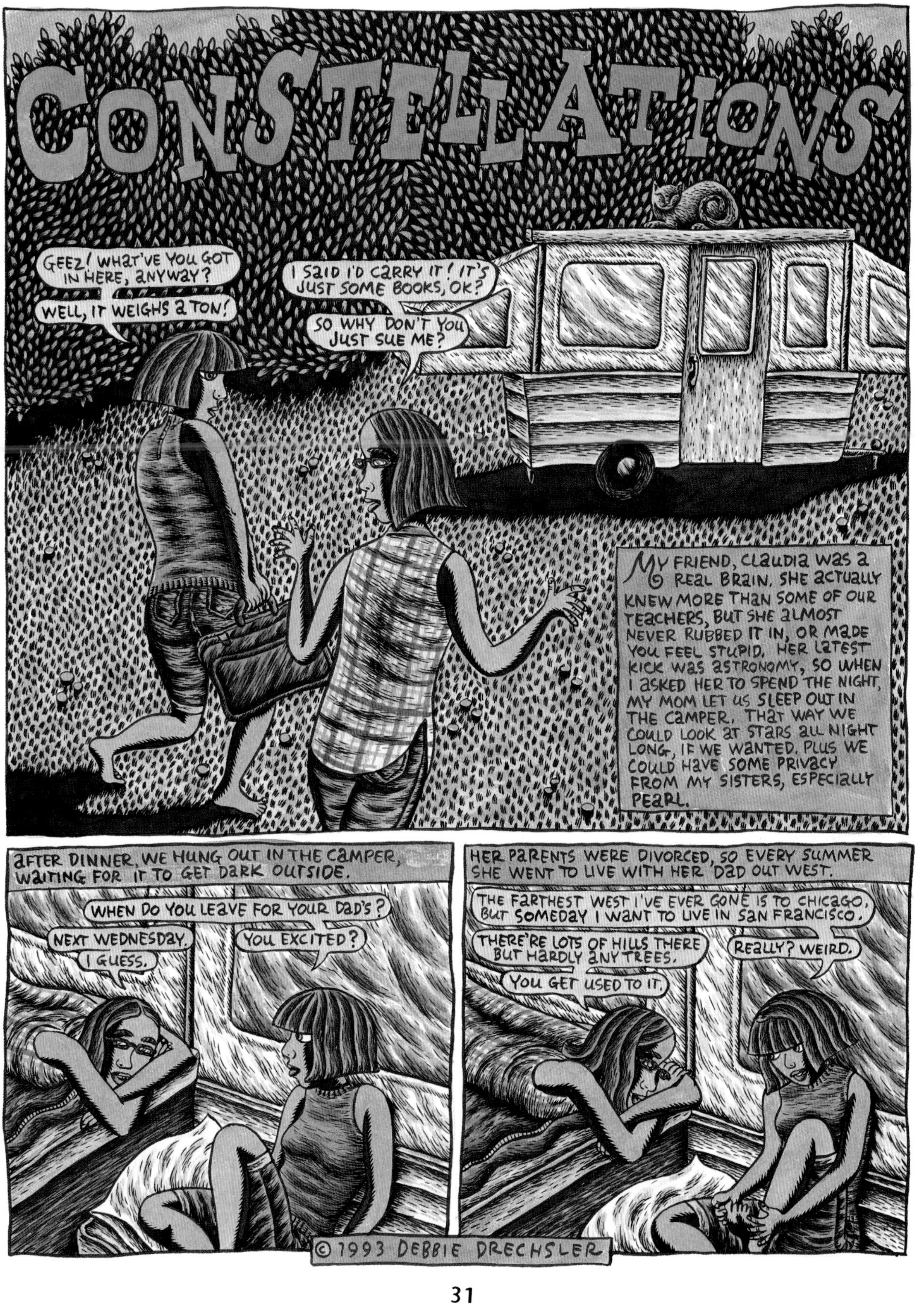
CONSTELLATIONS
GEEZ! WHAT'VE YOU GOT IN HERE, ANYWAY?
I SAID I'D CARRY IT! IT'S JUST SOME BOOKS, OK?
WELL, IT WEIGHS A TON!
SO WHY DON'T YOU JUST SUE ME?
MY FRIEND, CLAUDIA WAS A REAL BRAIN. SHE ACTUALLY KNEW MORE THAN SOME OF OUR TEACHERS, BUT SHE ALMOST NEVER RUBBED IT IN, OR MADE YOU FEEL STUPID. HER LATEST KICK WAS ASTRONOMY, SO WHEN I ASKED HER TO SPEND THE NIGHT, MY MOM LET US SLEEP OUT IN THE CAMPER. THAT WAY WE COULD LOOK AT STARS ALL NIGHT LONG, IF WE WANTED. PLUS WE COULD HAVE SOME PRIVACY FROM MY SISTERS, ESPECIALLY PEARL.
AFTER DINNER, WE HUNG OUT IN THE CAMPER, WAITING FOR IT TO GET DARK OUTSIDE.
WHEN DO YOU LEAVE FOR YOUR DAD'S?
NEXT WEDNESDAY, I GUESS.
YOU EXCITED?
HER PARENTS WERE DIVORCED, SO EVERY SUMMER SHE WENT TO LIVE WITH HER DAD OUT WEST.
THE FARTHEST WEST I'VE EVER GONE IS TO CHICAGO, BUT SOMEDAY I WANT TO LIVE IN SAN FRANCISCO.
THERE'RE LOTS OF HILLS THERE BUT HARDLY ANY TREES.
REALLY? WEIRD.
YOU GET USED TO IT.
©1993 DEBBIE DRECHSLER

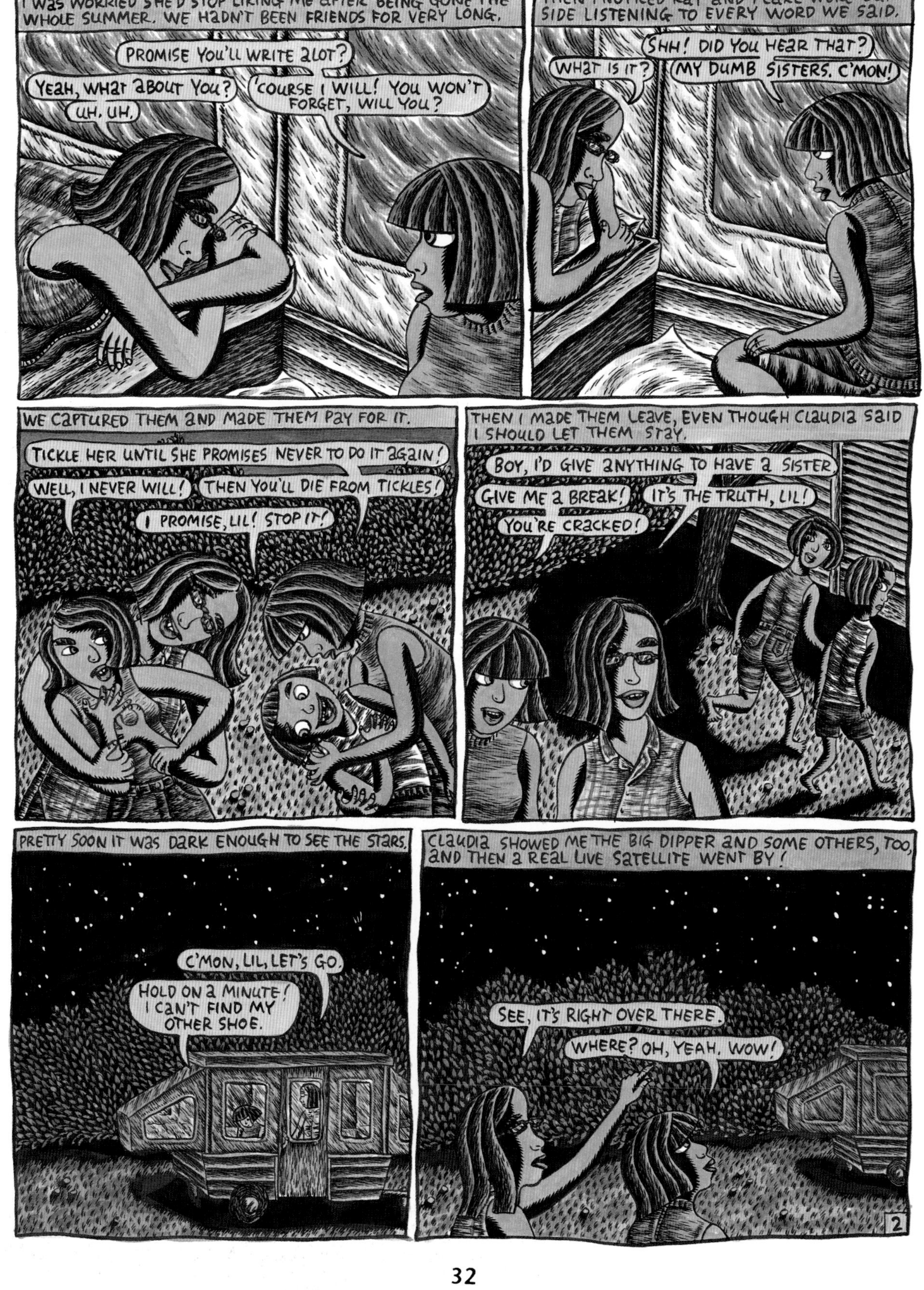
I WAS WORRIED SHE'D STOP LIKING ME AFTER BEING GONE THE WHOLE SUMMER. WE HADN'T BEEN FRIENDS FOR VERY LONG.
PROMISE YOU'LL WRITE ALOT?
YEAH, WHAT ABOUT YOU?
UH, UH.
'COURSE I WILL! YOU WON'T FORGET, WILL YOU?
THEN I NOTICED KAY AND PEARL WERE OUT-SIDE LISTENING TO EVERY WORD WE SAID.
SHH! DID YOU HEAR THAT?
WHAT IS IT?
MY DUMB SISTERS. C'MON!
WE CAPTURED THEM AND MADE THEM PAY FOR IT.
TICKLE HER UNTIL SHE PROMISES NEVER TO DO IT AGAIN!
WELL, I NEVER WILL!
THEN YOU'LL DIE FROM TICKLES!
I PROMISE, LIL! STOP IT!
THEN I MADE THEM LEAVE, EVEN THOUGH CLAUDIA SAID I SHOULD LET THEM STAY.
BOY, I'D GIVE ANYTHING TO HAVE A SISTER.
GIVE ME A BREAK!
IT'S THE TRUTH, LIL!
YOU'RE CRACKED!
PRETTY SOON IT WAS DARK ENOUGH TO SEE THE STARS.
C'MON, LIL, LET'S GO.
HOLD ON A MINUTE! I CAN'T FIND MY OTHER SHOE.
CLAUDIA SHOWED ME THE BIG DIPPER AND SOME OTHERS, TOO, AND THEN A REAL LIVE SATELLITE WENT BY!
SEE, IT'S RIGHT OVER THERE.
WHERE? OH, YEAH, WOW!
2

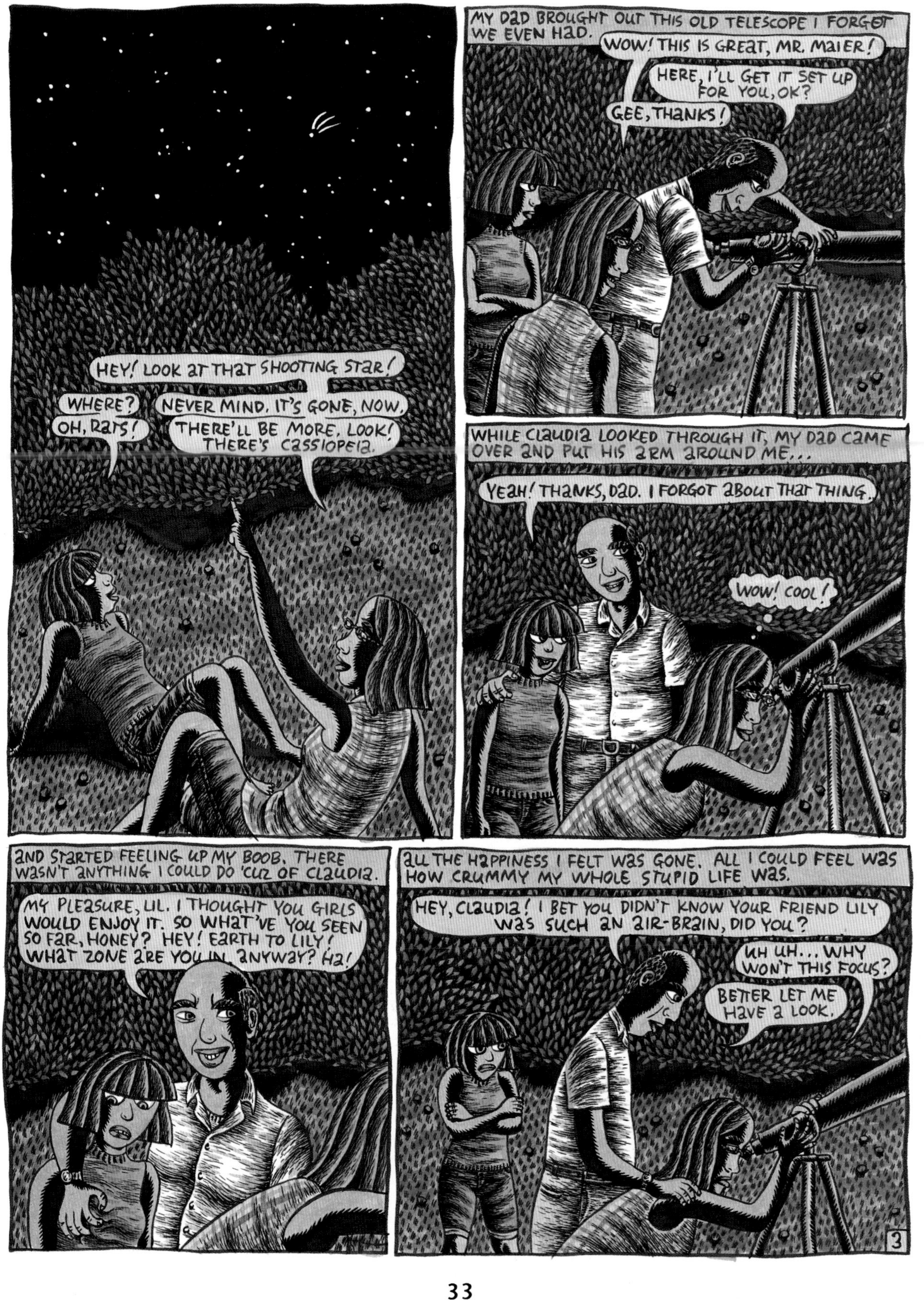
HEY! LOOK AT THAT SHOOTING STAR!
WHERE? OH, RATS!
NEVER MIND. IT'S GONE, NOW. THERE'LL BE MORE, LOOK! THERE'S CASSIOPEIA.
MY DAD BROUGHT OUT THIS OLD TELESCOPE I FORGOT WE EVEN HAD.
WOW! THIS IS GREAT, MR. MAIER!
HERE, I'LL GET IT SET UP FOR YOU, OK?
GEE, THANKS!
WHILE CLAUDIA LOOKED THROUGH IT, MY DAD CAME OVER AND PUT HIS ARM AROUND ME...
YEAH! THANKS, DAD. I FORGOT ABOUT THAT THING.
WOW! COOL!
AND STARTED FEELING UP MY BOOB. THERE WASN'T ANYTHING I COULD DO 'CUZ OF CLAUDIA.
MY PLEASURE, LIL. I THOUGHT YOU GIRLS WOULD ENJOY IT. SO WHAT'VE YOU SEEN SO FAR, HONEY? HEY! EARTH TO LILY! WHAT ZONE ARE YOU IN, ANYWAY? HA!
ALL THE HAPPINESS I FELT WAS GONE. ALL I COULD FEEL WAS HOW CRUMMY MY WHOLE STUPID LIFE WAS.
HEY, CLAUDIA! I BET YOU DIDN'T KNOW YOUR FRIEND LILY WAS SUCH AN AIR-BRAIN, DID YOU?
UH UH... WHY WON'T THIS FOCUS?
BETTER LET ME HAVE A LOOK.
3

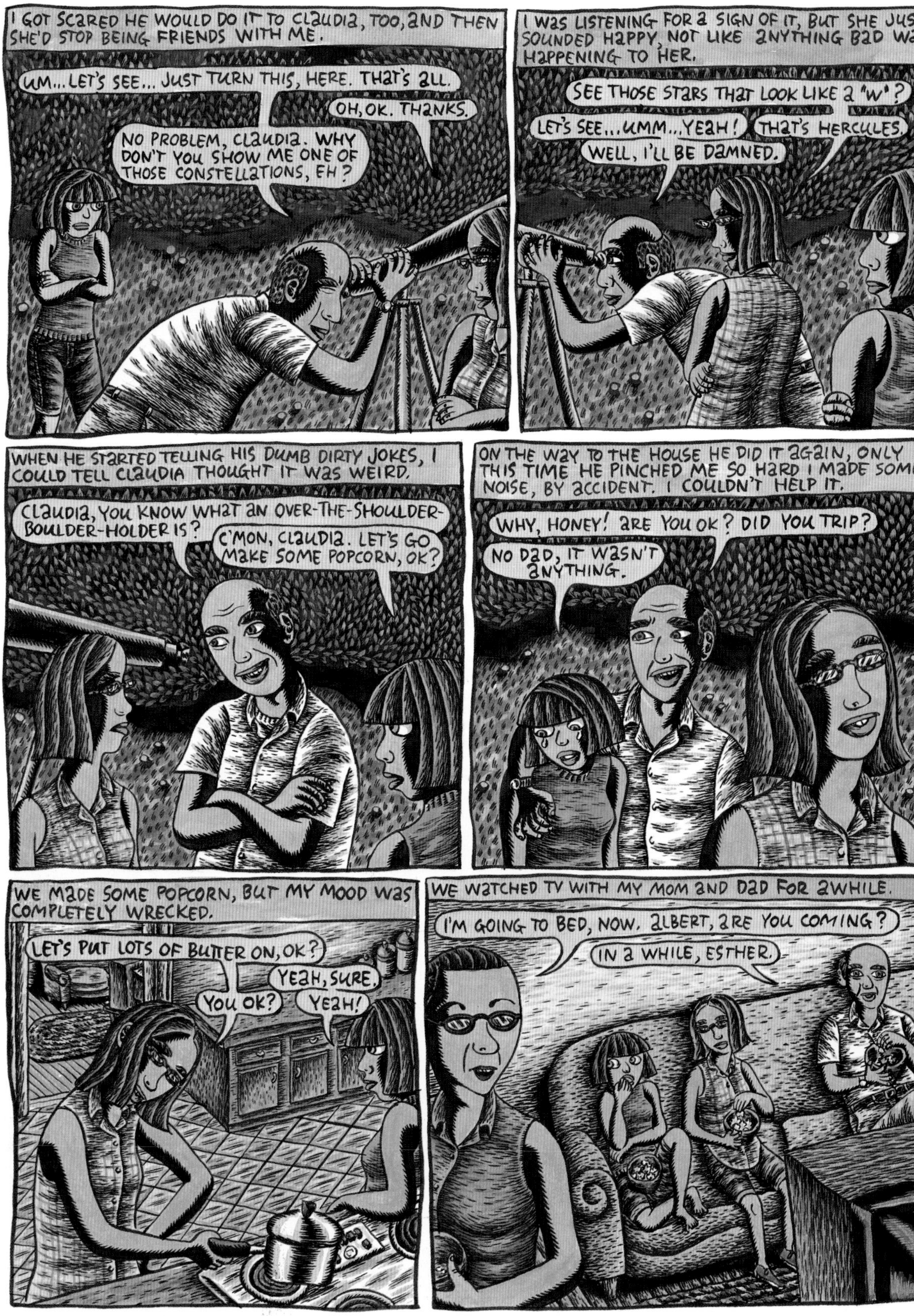
I GOT SCARED HE WOULD DO IT TO CLAUDIA, TOO, AND THEN SHE'D STOP BEING FRIENDS WITH ME.
UM... LET'S SEE... JUST TURN THIS, HERE. THAT'S ALL.
OH, OK. THANKS.
NO PROBLEM, CLAUDIA. WHY DON'T YOU SHOW ME ONE OF THOSE CONSTELLATIONS, EH?
I WAS LISTENING FOR A SIGN OF IT, BUT SHE JUST SOUNDED HAPPY, NOT LIKE ANYTHING BAD WAS HAPPENING TO HER.
SEE THOSE STARS THAT LOOK LIKE A "W"?
LET'S SEE... UMM... YEAH!
THAT'S HERCULES.
WELL, I'LL BE DAMNED.
WHEN HE STARTED TELLING HIS DUMB DIRTY JOKES, I COULD TELL CLAUDIA THOUGHT IT WAS WEIRD.
CLAUDIA, YOU KNOW WHAT AN OVER-THE-SHOULDER-BOULDER-HOLDER IS?
C'MON, CLAUDIA. LET'S GO MAKE SOME POPCORN, OK?
ON THE WAY TO THE HOUSE HE DID IT AGAIN, ONLY THIS TIME HE PINCHED ME SO HARD I MADE SOME NOISE, BY ACCIDENT. I COULDN'T HELP IT.
WHY, HONEY! ARE YOU OK? DID YOU TRIP?
NO DAD, IT WASN'T ANYTHING.
WE MADE SOME POPCORN, BUT MY MOOD WAS COMPLETELY WRECKED.
LET'S PUT LOTS OF BUTTER ON, OK?
YEAH, SURE.
YOU OK?
YEAH!
WE WATCHED TV WITH MY MOM AND DAD FOR AWHILE.
I'M GOING TO BED, NOW. ALBERT, ARE YOU COMING?
IN A WHILE, ESTHER.
4

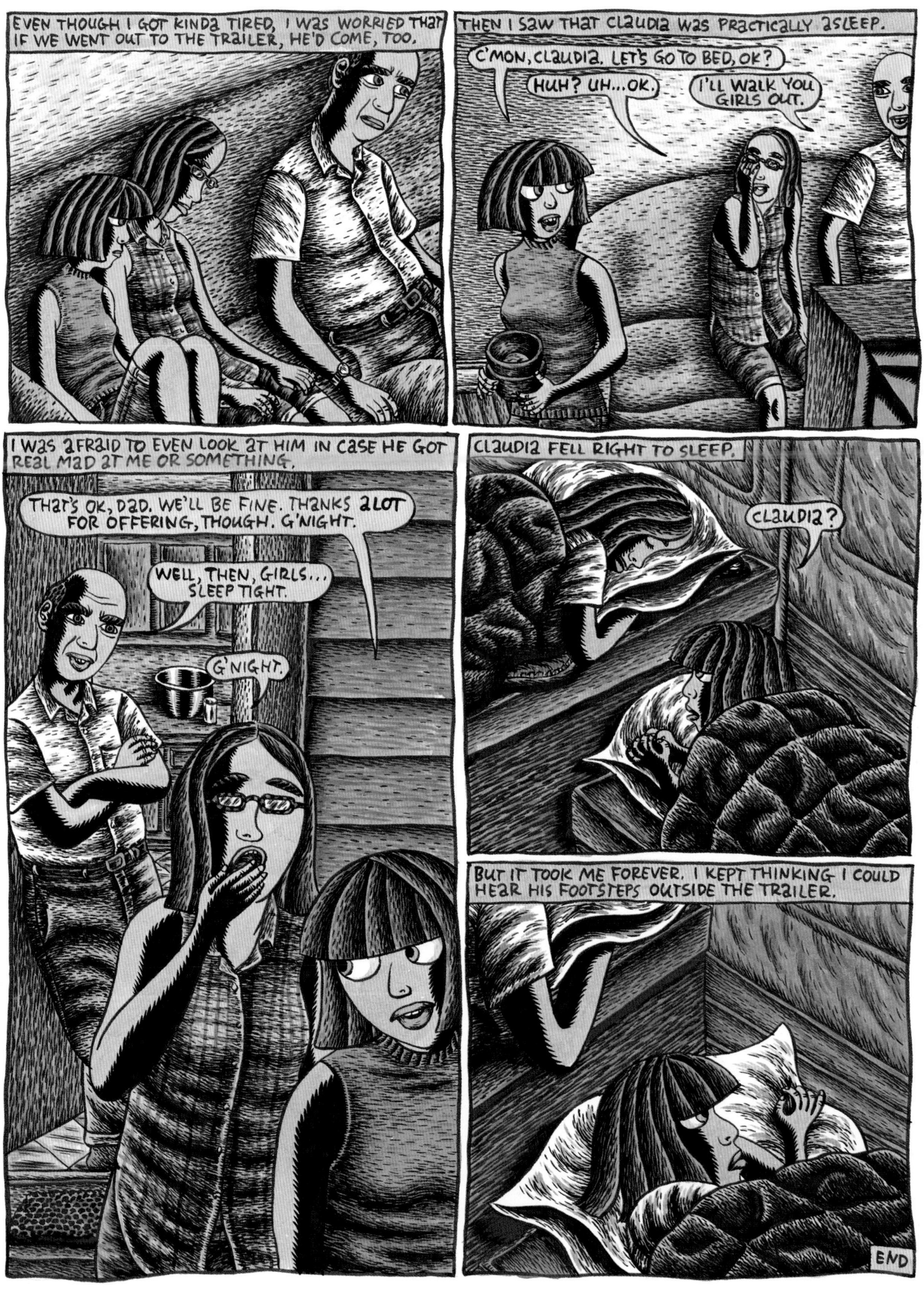
EVEN THOUGH I GOT KINDA TIRED, I WAS WORRIED THAT IF WE WENT OUT TO THE TRAILER, HE'D COME, TOO.
THEN I SAW THAT CLAUDIA WAS PRACTICALLY ASLEEP.
C'MON, CLAUDIA. LET'S GO TO BED, OK?
HUH? UH...OK.
I'LL WALK YOU GIRLS OUT.
I WAS AFRAID TO EVEN LOOK AT HIM IN CASE HE GOT REAL MAD AT ME OR SOMETHING.
THAT'S OK, DAD. WE'LL BE FINE. THANKS ALOT FOR OFFERING, THOUGH. G'NIGHT.
WELL, THEN, GIRLS... SLEEP TIGHT.
G'NIGHT.
CLAUDIA FELL RIGHT TO SLEEP.
CLAUDIA?
BUT IT TOOK ME FOREVER. I KEPT THINKING I COULD HEAR HIS FOOTSTEPS OUTSIDE THE TRAILER.
END

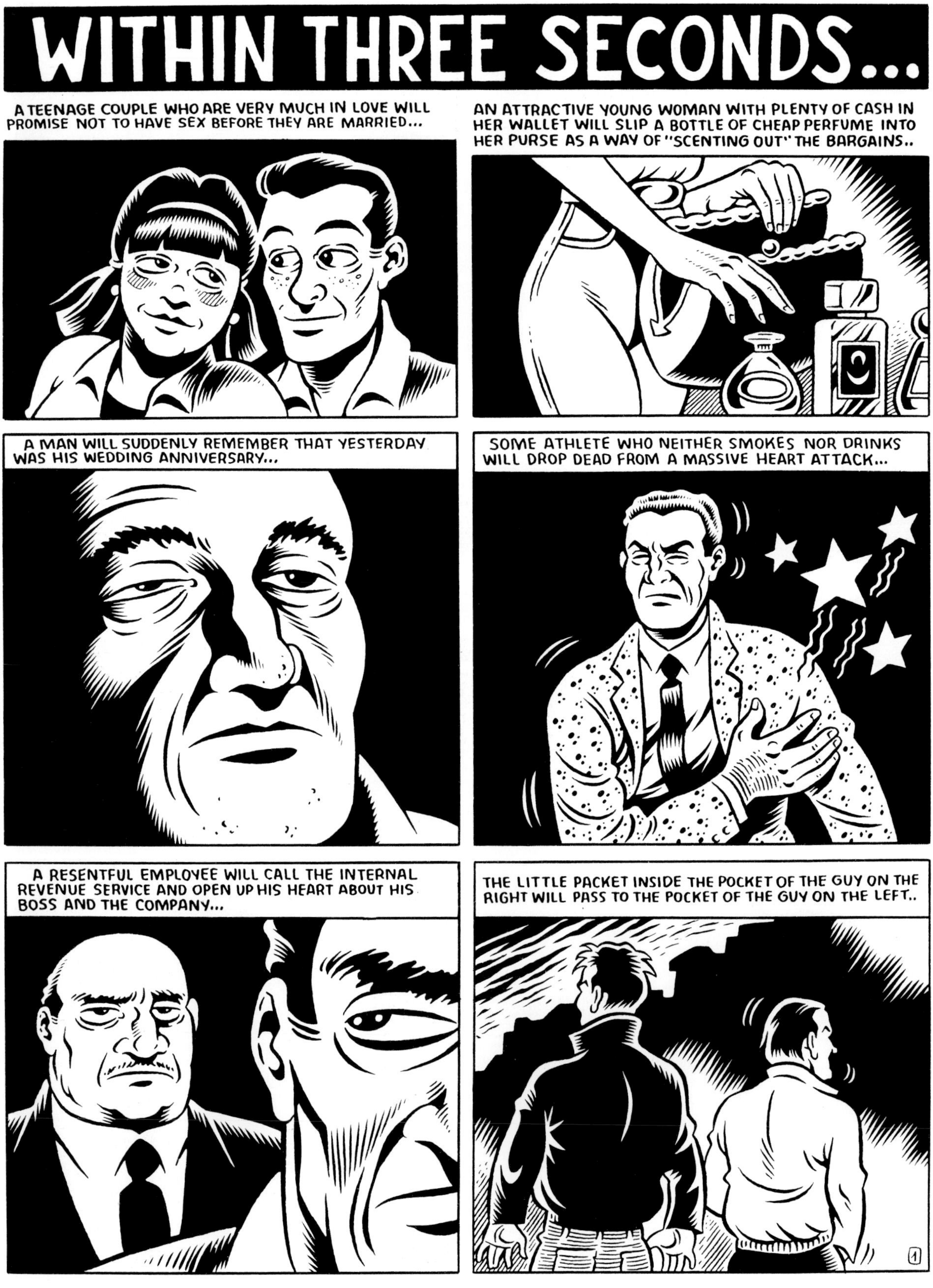
WITHIN THREE SECONDS...
A TEENAGE COUPLE WHO ARE VERY MUCH IN LOVE WILL PROMISE NOT TO HAVE SEX BEFORE THEY ARE MARRIED...
AN ATTRACTIVE YOUNG WOMAN WITH PLENTY OF CASH IN HER WALLET WILL SLIP A BOTTLE OF CHEAP PERFUME INTO HER PURSE AS A WAY OF "SCENTING OUT" THE BARGAINS..
A MAN WILL SUDDENLY REMEMBER THAT YESTERDAY WAS HIS WEDDING ANNIVERSARY...
SOME ATHLETE WHO NEITHER SMOKES NOR DRINKS WILL DROP DEAD FROM A MASSIVE HEART ATTACK...
A RESENTFUL EMPLOYEE WILL CALL THE INTERNAL REVENUE SERVICE AND OPEN UP HIS HEART ABOUT HIS BOSS AND THE COMPANY...
THE LITTLE PACKET INSIDE THE POCKET OF THE GUY ON THE RIGHT WILL PASS TO THE POCKET OF THE GUY ON THE LEFT..
1

A MIDDLE MAN WILL CLOSE A REAL ESTATE DEAL BY TELEPHONE AND WILL HAVE EARNED HIMSELF A COOL 250 GRAND BY THE TIME HE HANGS UP...

SOME CLOWN WILL BUTT OUT YET ANOTHER CIGARETTE ON THE BODY OF HIS SIX-MONTH OLD BABY...

A MAN FROM SENEGAL WILL ASK AN OLD WOMAN THE TIME AND SEND HER INTO HYSTERICS...

A CATALAN WILL APPLY TWO HUNDRED AND TWENTY VOLTS TO HIS GENITALS AND FINALLY REACH WILD ORGASM AFTER MUCH MASTURBATION...

AN INDUSTRIAL ENGINEER WILL CONNECT THE LAST CIRCUIT ON A TIME BOMB CONTAINING ONE HUNDRED POUNDS OF EXPLOSIVES...

SOME JUDGE WILL REACH THE CONCLUSION THAT HIS CONSTIPATION ISN'T GETTING ANY BETTER...

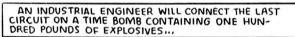

ONE...TWO...THREE!!

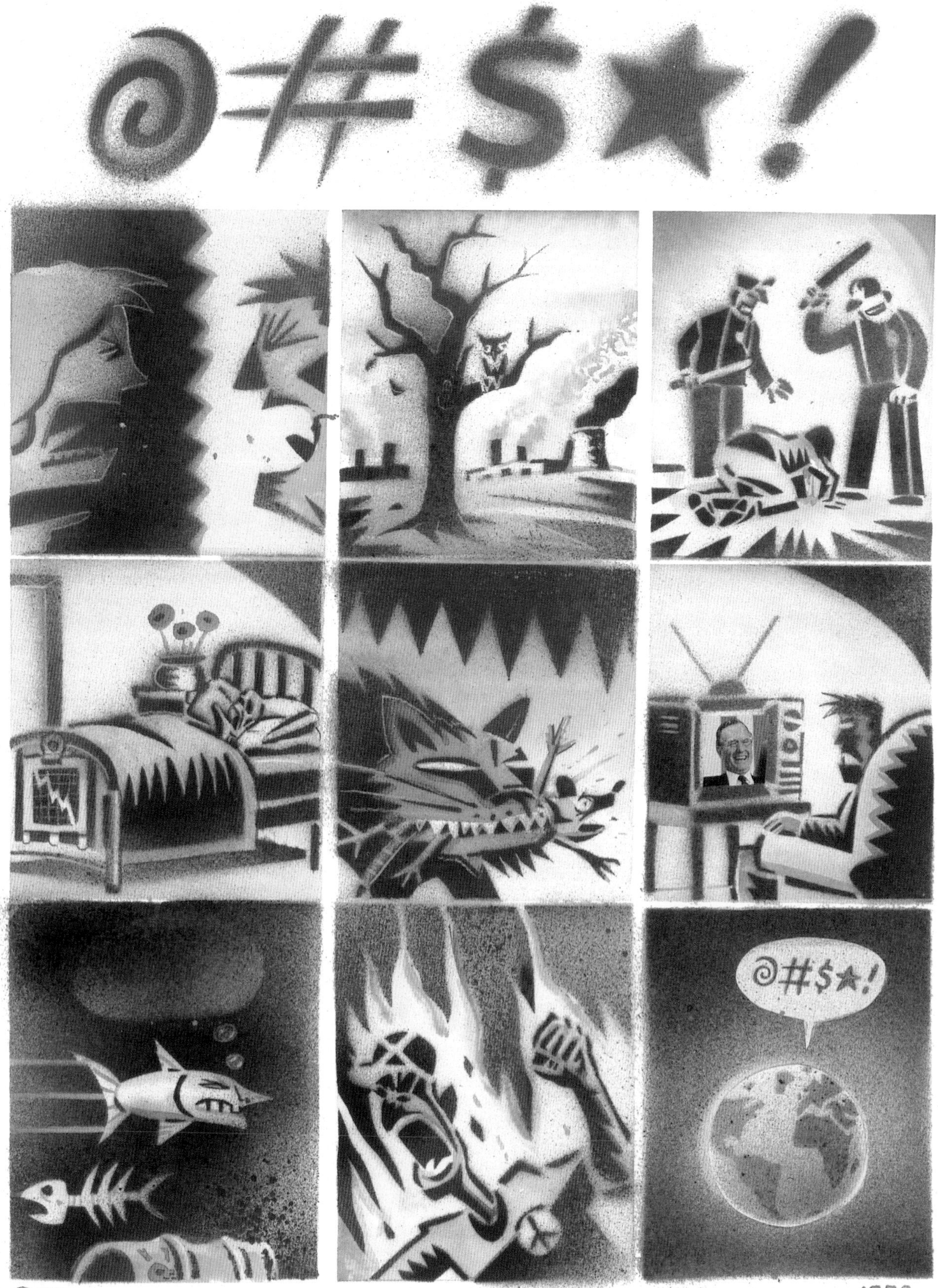
@#$★!
@#$★!

© PETER KUPER 1992

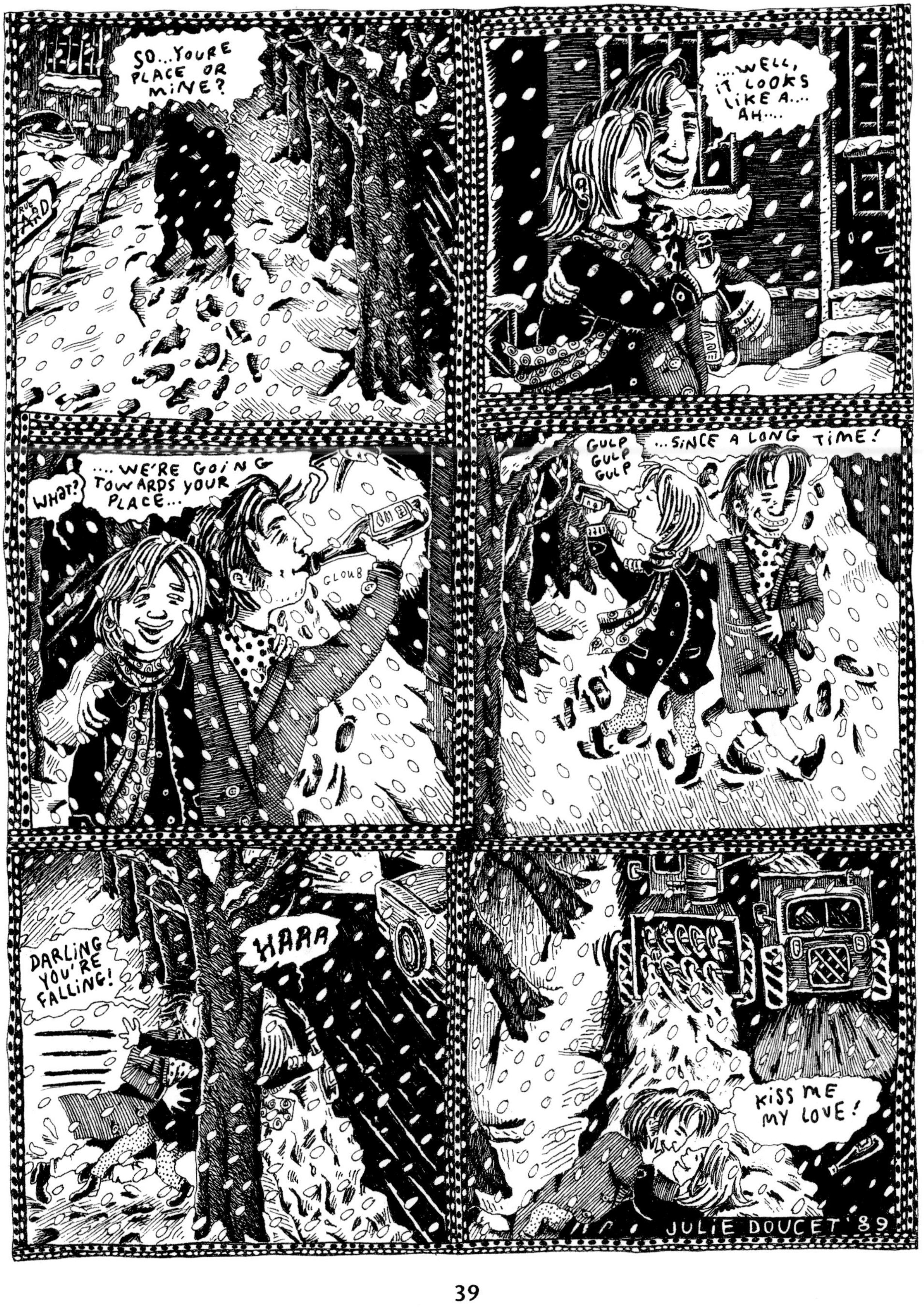
SO... YOURE PLACE OR MINE?
RUE ... ARD
...WELL, IT LOOKS LIKE A.... AH....
WHAT?
....WE'RE GOING TOWARDS YOUR PLACE...
GLOUB
GULP GULP GULP
...SINCE A LONG TIME!
DARLING YOU'RE FALLING!
HARA
KISS ME MY LOVE!
JULIE DOUCET '89

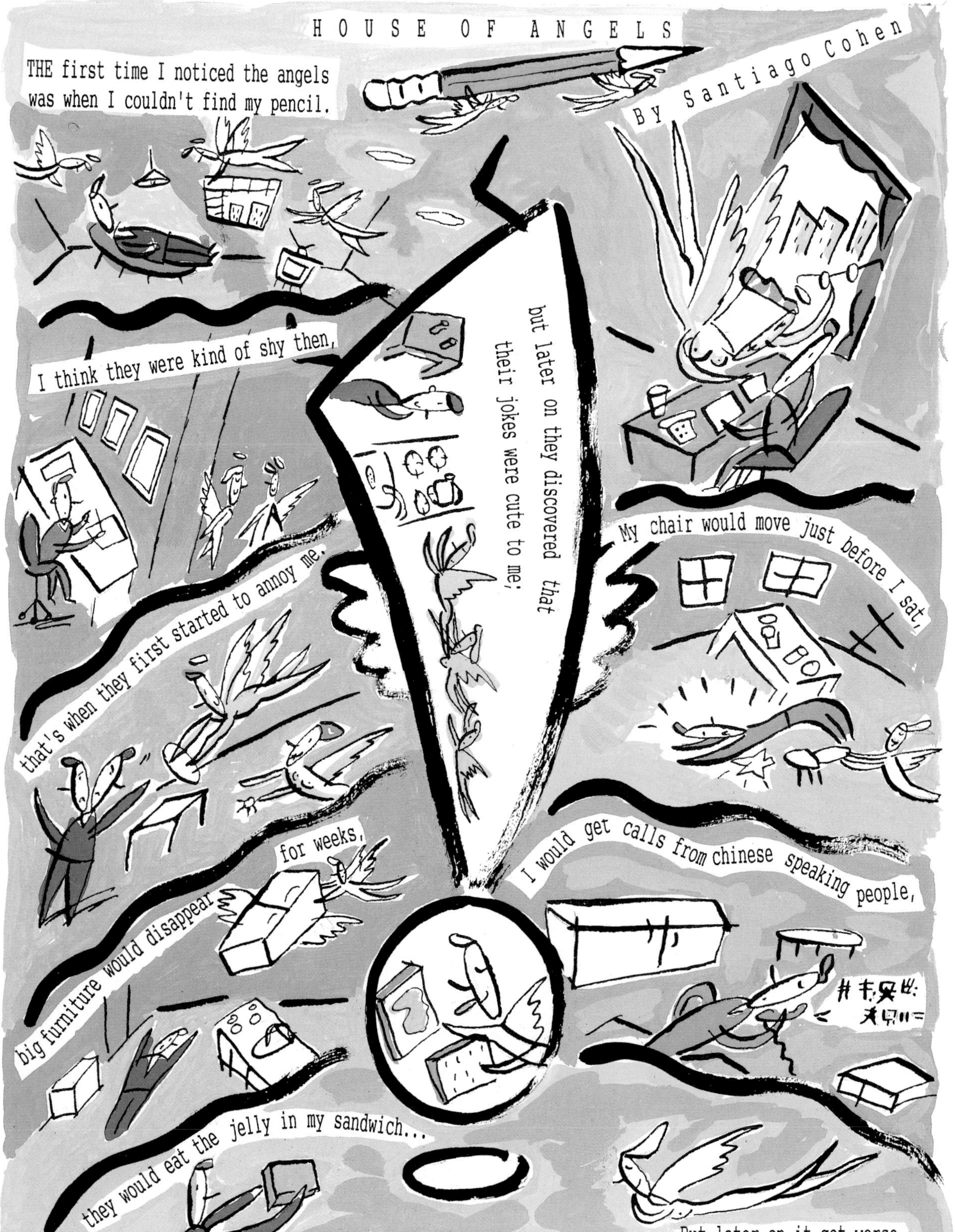
HOUSE OF ANGELS
By Santiago Cohen
THE first time I noticed the angels was when I couldn't find my pencil.
I think they were kind of shy then,
but later on they discovered that their jokes were cute to me;
My chair would move just before I sat,
that's when they first started to annoy me.
big furniture would disappear for weeks,
I would get calls from chinese speaking people,
they would eat the jelly in my sandwich...
But later on it got worse,

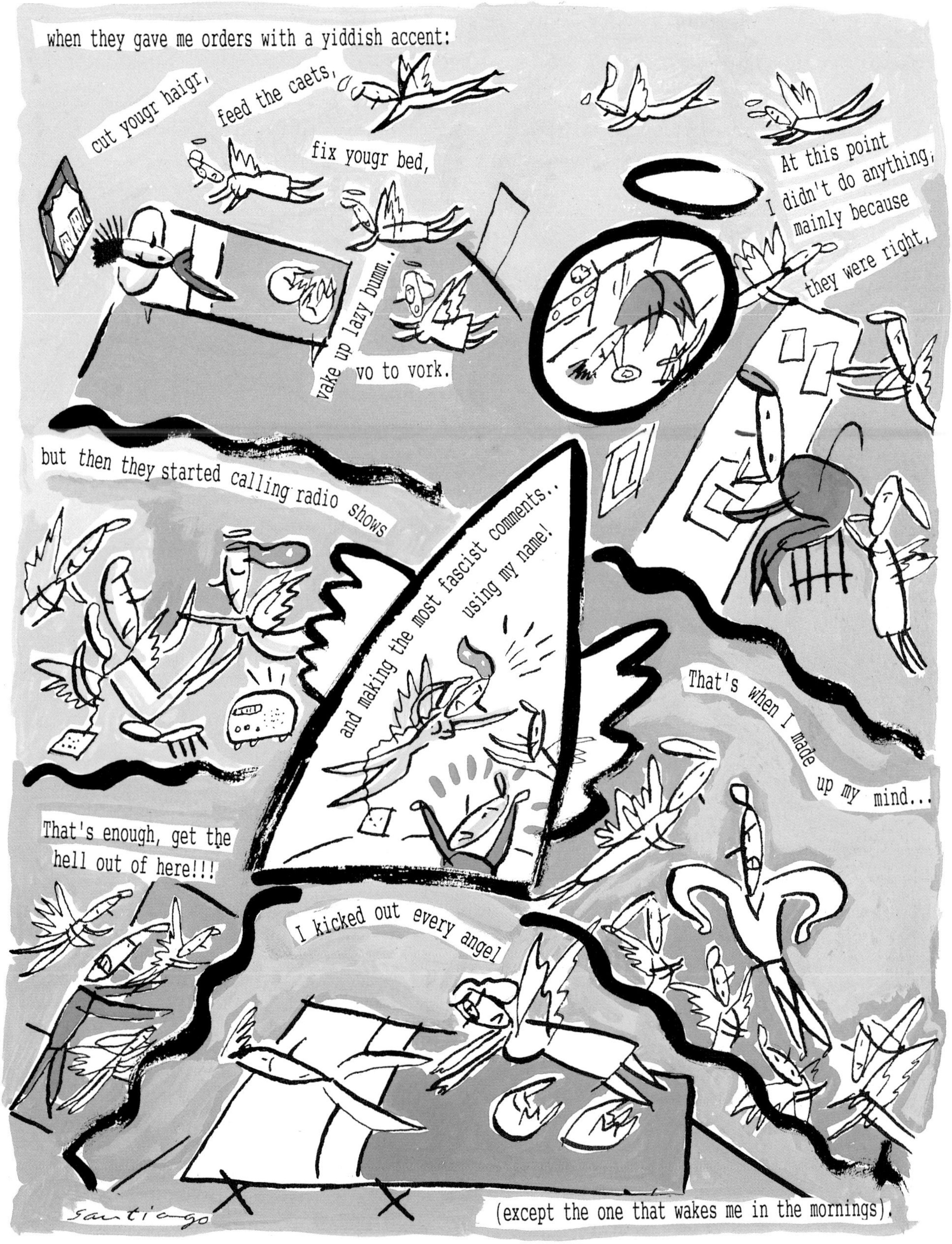
when they gave me orders with a yiddish accent:
cut yougr haigr,
feed the caets,
fix yougr bed,
vake up lazy bumm..
vo to vork.
At this point I didn't do anything, mainly because they were right,
but then they started calling radio shows
and making the most fascist comments..
using my name!
That's when I made up my mind...
That's enough, get the hell out of here!!!
I kicked out every angel
(except the one that wakes me in the mornings).
santiago

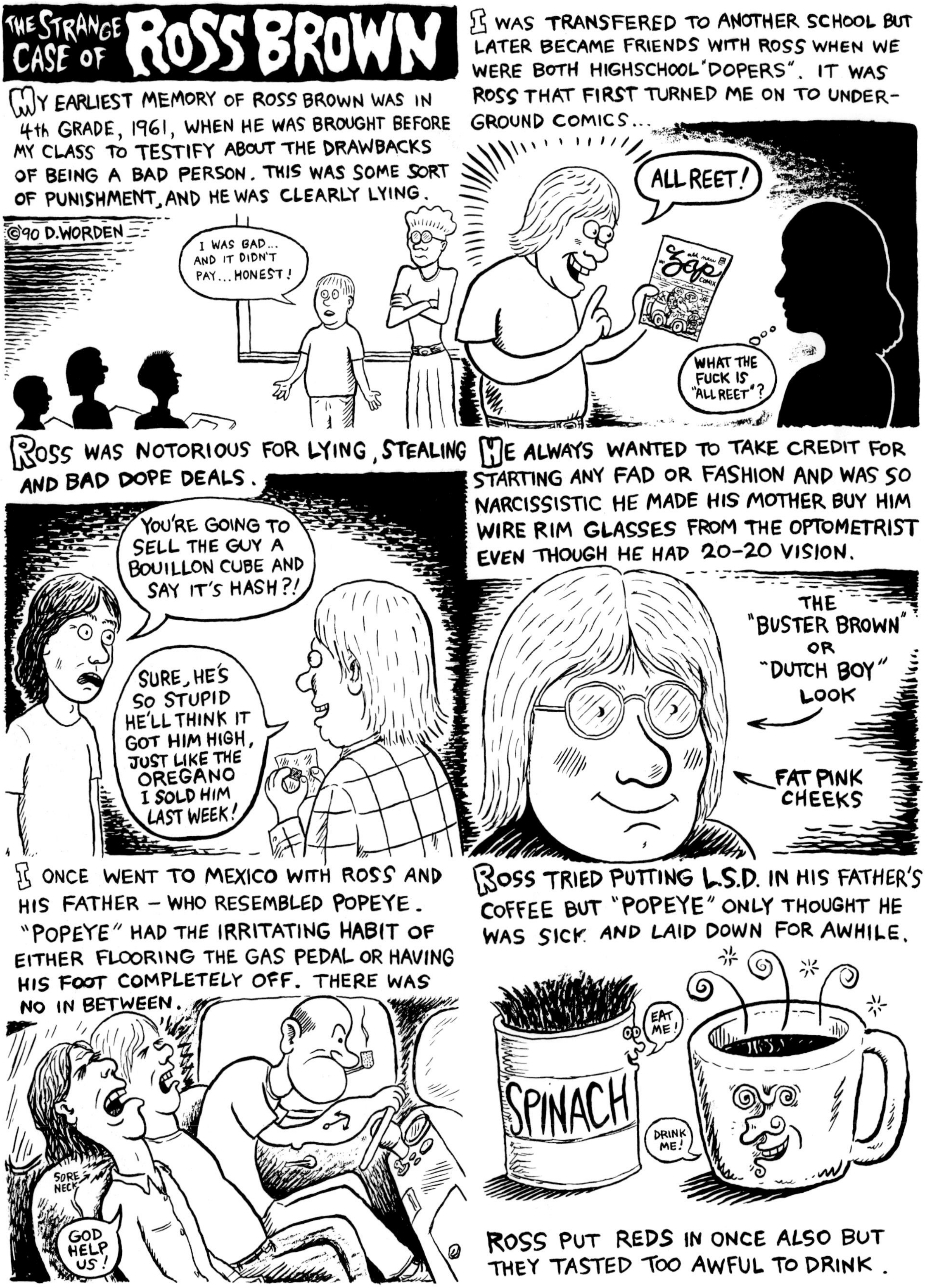
THE STRANGE CASE OF ROSS BROWN
MY EARLIEST MEMORY OF ROSS BROWN WAS IN 4th GRADE, 1961, WHEN HE WAS BROUGHT BEFORE MY CLASS TO TESTIFY ABOUT THE DRAWBACKS OF BEING A BAD PERSON. THIS WAS SOME SORT OF PUNISHMENT, AND HE WAS CLEARLY LYING.
©90 D.WORDEN
I WAS BAD... AND IT DIDN'T PAY... HONEST!
I WAS TRANSFERED TO ANOTHER SCHOOL BUT LATER BECAME FRIENDS WITH ROSS WHEN WE WERE BOTH HIGHSCHOOL "DOPERS". IT WAS ROSS THAT FIRST TURNED ME ON TO UNDERGROUND COMICS...
ALL REET!
WHAT THE FUCK IS "ALL REET"?
ROSS WAS NOTORIOUS FOR LYING, STEALING AND BAD DOPE DEALS.
YOU'RE GOING TO SELL THE GUY A BOUILLON CUBE AND SAY IT'S HASH?!
SURE, HE'S SO STUPID HE'LL THINK IT GOT HIM HIGH, JUST LIKE THE OREGANO I SOLD HIM LAST WEEK!
HE ALWAYS WANTED TO TAKE CREDIT FOR STARTING ANY FAD OR FASHION AND WAS SO NARCISSISTIC HE MADE HIS MOTHER BUY HIM WIRE RIM GLASSES FROM THE OPTOMETRIST EVEN THOUGH HE HAD 20-20 VISION.
THE "BUSTER BROWN" OR "DUTCH BOY" LOOK
FAT PINK CHEEKS
I ONCE WENT TO MEXICO WITH ROSS AND HIS FATHER - WHO RESEMBLED POPEYE. "POPEYE" HAD THE IRRITATING HABIT OF EITHER FLOORING THE GAS PEDAL OR HAVING HIS FOOT COMPLETELY OFF. THERE WAS NO IN BETWEEN.
SORE NECK
GOD HELP US!
ROSS TRIED PUTTING L.S.D. IN HIS FATHER'S COFFEE BUT "POPEYE" ONLY THOUGHT HE WAS SICK AND LAID DOWN FOR AWHILE.
EAT ME!
SPINACH
DRINK ME!
ROSS PUT REDS IN ONCE ALSO BUT THEY TASTED TOO AWFUL TO DRINK.

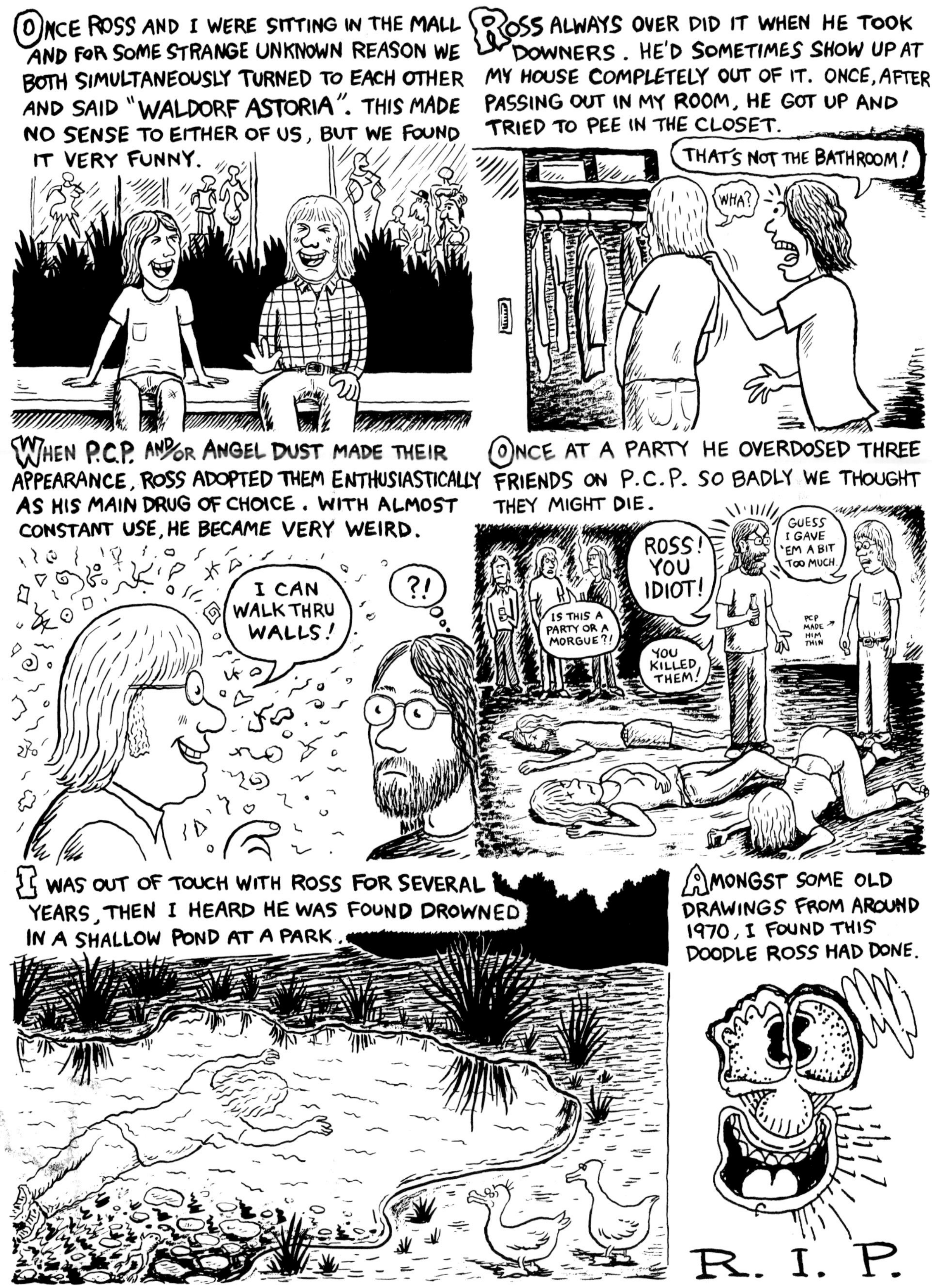
ONCE ROSS AND I WERE SITTING IN THE MALL AND FOR SOME STRANGE UNKNOWN REASON WE BOTH SIMULTANEOUSLY TURNED TO EACH OTHER AND SAID "WALDORF ASTORIA". THIS MADE NO SENSE TO EITHER OF US, BUT WE FOUND IT VERY FUNNY.
ROSS ALWAYS OVER DID IT WHEN HE TOOK DOWNERS. HE'D SOMETIMES SHOW UP AT MY HOUSE COMPLETELY OUT OF IT. ONCE, AFTER PASSING OUT IN MY ROOM, HE GOT UP AND TRIED TO PEE IN THE CLOSET.
THAT'S NOT THE BATHROOM!
WHA?
WHEN P.C.P. AND/OR ANGEL DUST MADE THEIR APPEARANCE, ROSS ADOPTED THEM ENTHUSIASTICALLY AS HIS MAIN DRUG OF CHOICE. WITH ALMOST CONSTANT USE, HE BECAME VERY WEIRD.
I CAN WALK THRU WALLS!
?!
ONCE AT A PARTY HE OVERDOSED THREE FRIENDS ON P.C.P. SO BADLY WE THOUGHT THEY MIGHT DIE.
IS THIS A PARTY OR A MORGUE?!
ROSS! YOU IDIOT!
YOU KILLED THEM!
GUESS I GAVE 'EM A BIT TOO MUCH.
PCP MADE HIM THIN
I WAS OUT OF TOUCH WITH ROSS FOR SEVERAL YEARS, THEN I HEARD HE WAS FOUND DROWNED IN A SHALLOW POND AT A PARK.
AMONGST SOME OLD DRAWINGS FROM AROUND 1970, I FOUND THIS DOODLE ROSS HAD DONE.
R. I. P.

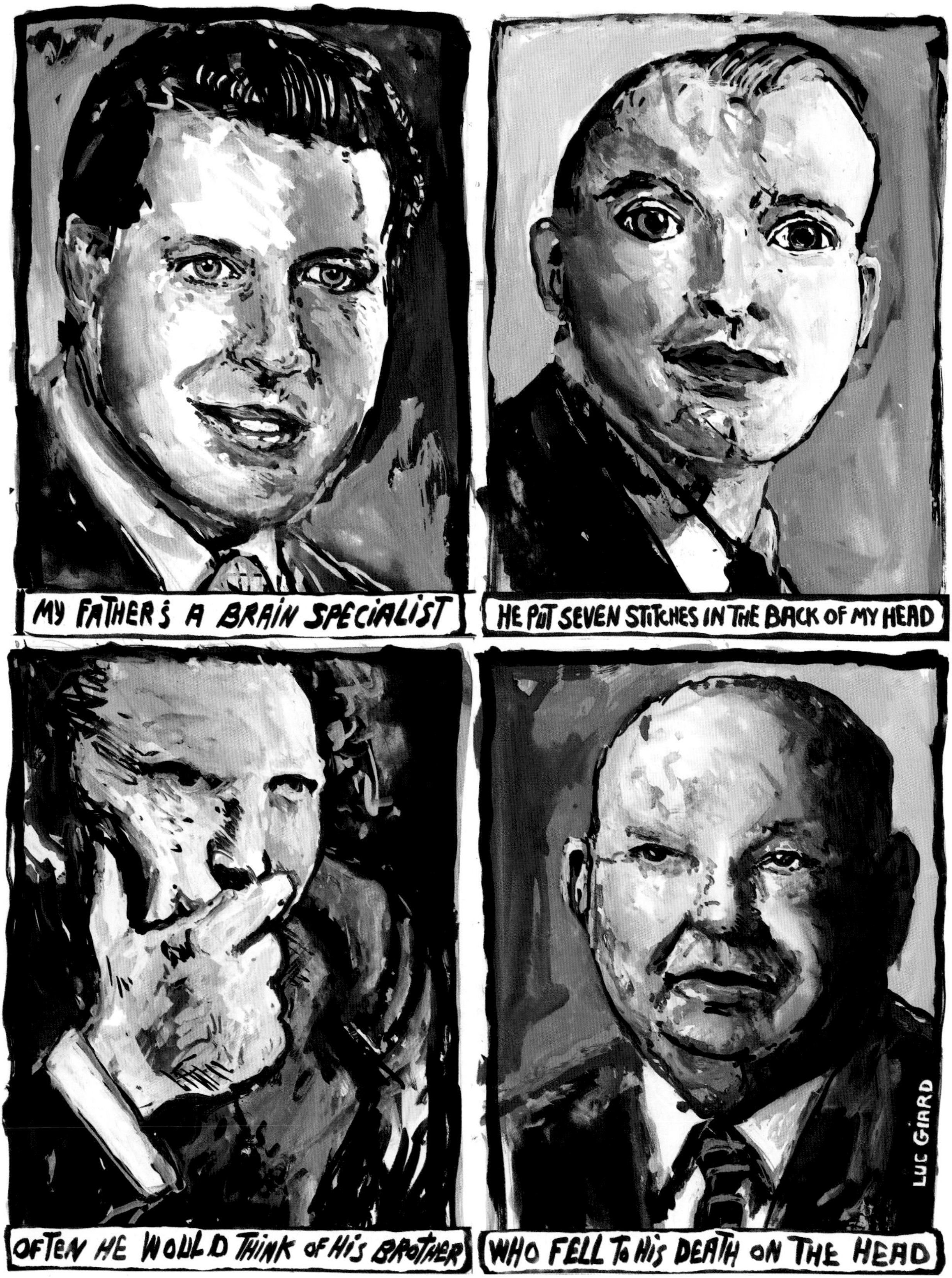
MY FATHER'S A BRAIN SPECIALIST
HE PUT SEVEN STITCHES IN THE BACK OF MY HEAD
OFTEN HE WOULD THINK OF HIS BROTHER
WHO FELL TO HIS DEATH ON THE HEAD
LUC GIARD

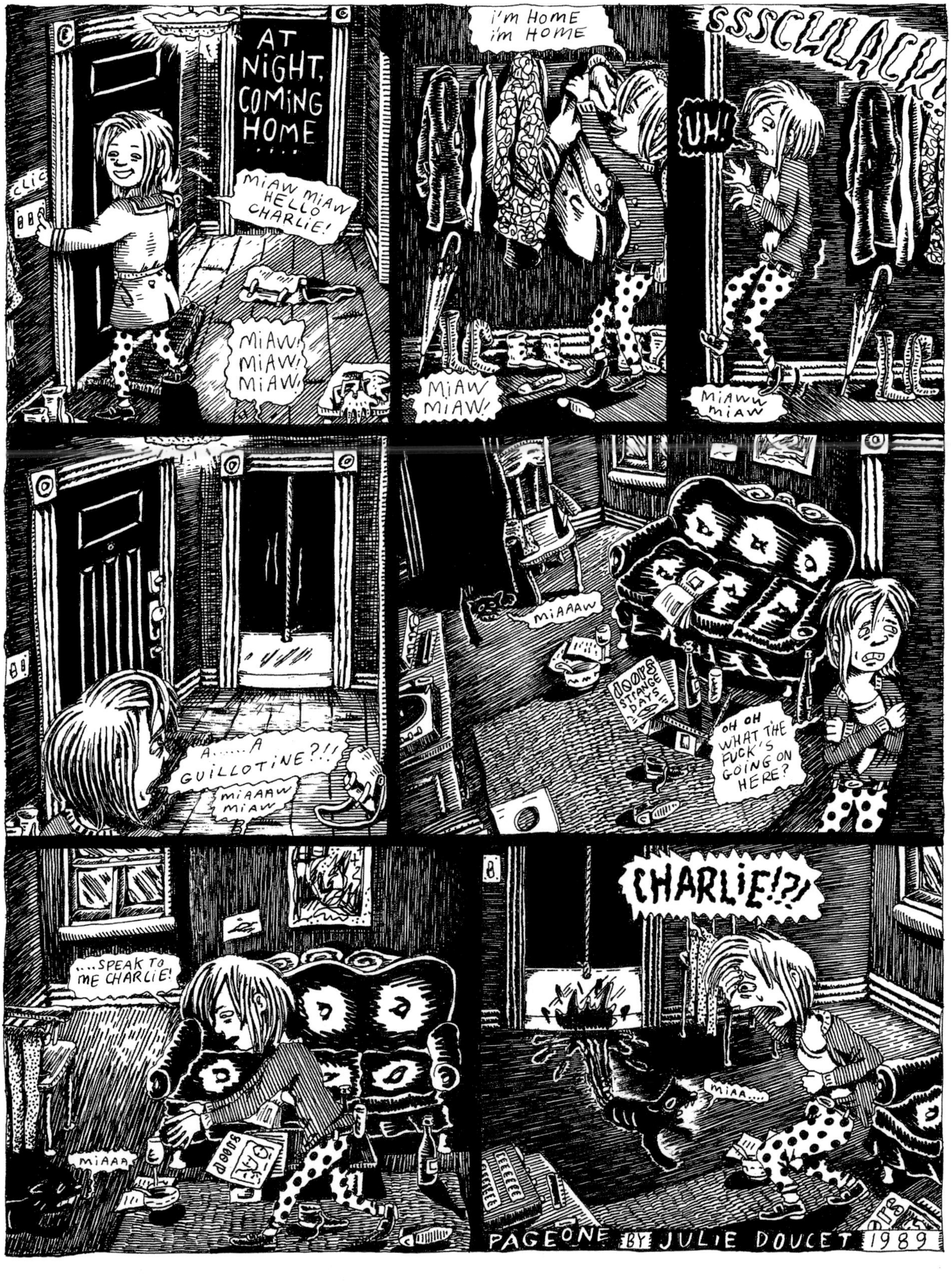

AT NIGHT, COMING HOME ....
CLIC
MIAW MIAW HELLO CHARLIE!
MIAW! MIAW! MIAW!
I'M HOME I'M HOME
MIAW MIAW!
SSSCHLACK!
UH!
MIAWW MIAW
A...... A GUILLOTINE?!!
MIAAAW MIAW
MIAAAW
doors STRANGE DAYS
OH OH WHAT THE FUCK'S GOING ON HERE?
....SPEAK TO ME CHARLIE!
MIAAA
CHARLIE!?!
MIAA....
PAGEONE BY JULIE DOUCET 1989

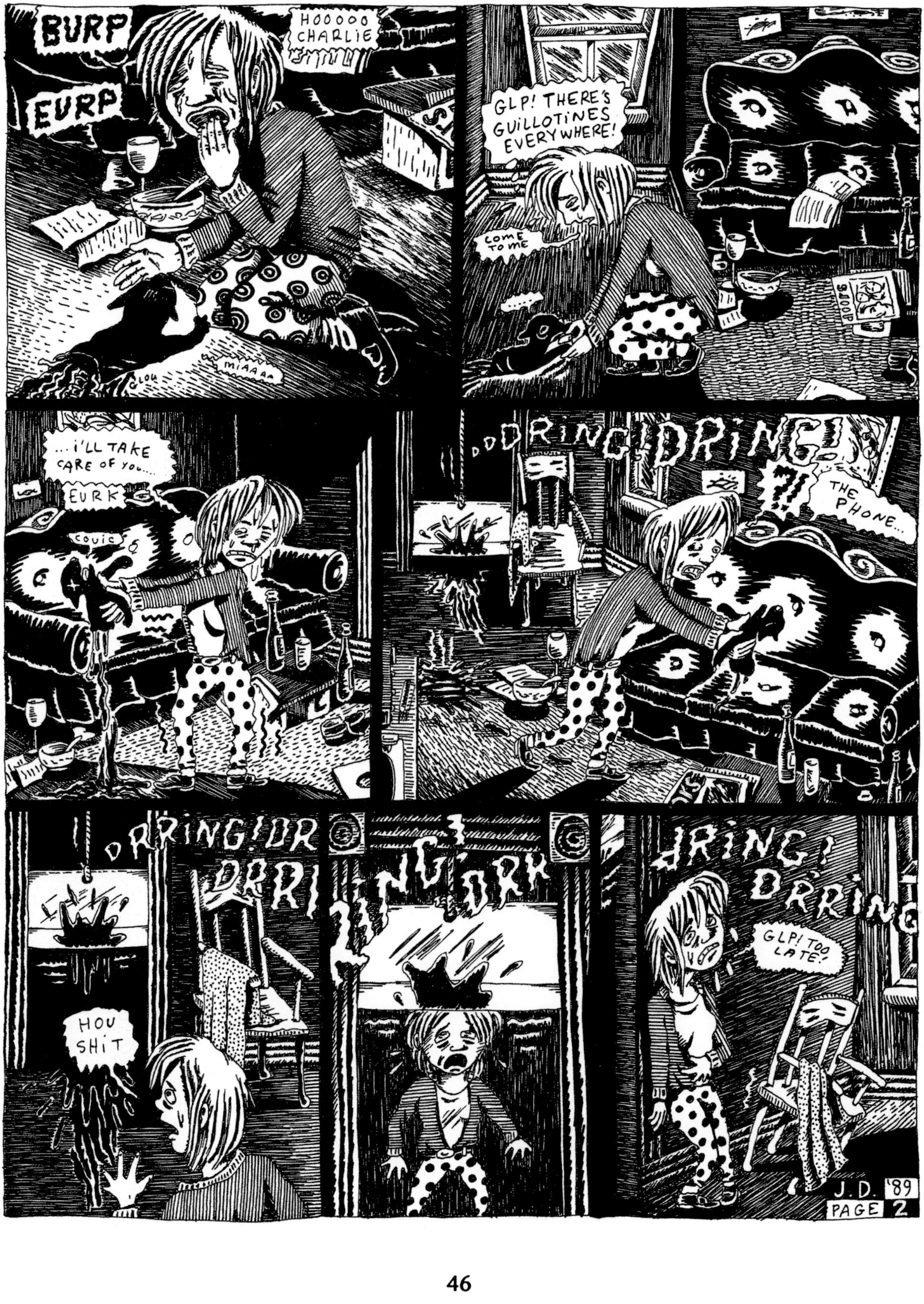
BURP
EVRP
HOOOOO CHARLIE
GLOU
MIAAAAA
GLP! THERE'S GUILLOTINES EVERYWHERE!
COME TO ME
...
...I'LL TAKE CARE OF YOU...
EURK
COUIC
DDDRING! DRING!
?!
THE PHONE...
DRRING! DR
DRRING! DRK
HOU SHIT
DRING!
DRRING
GLP! TOO LATE!
J.D. '89
PAGE 2

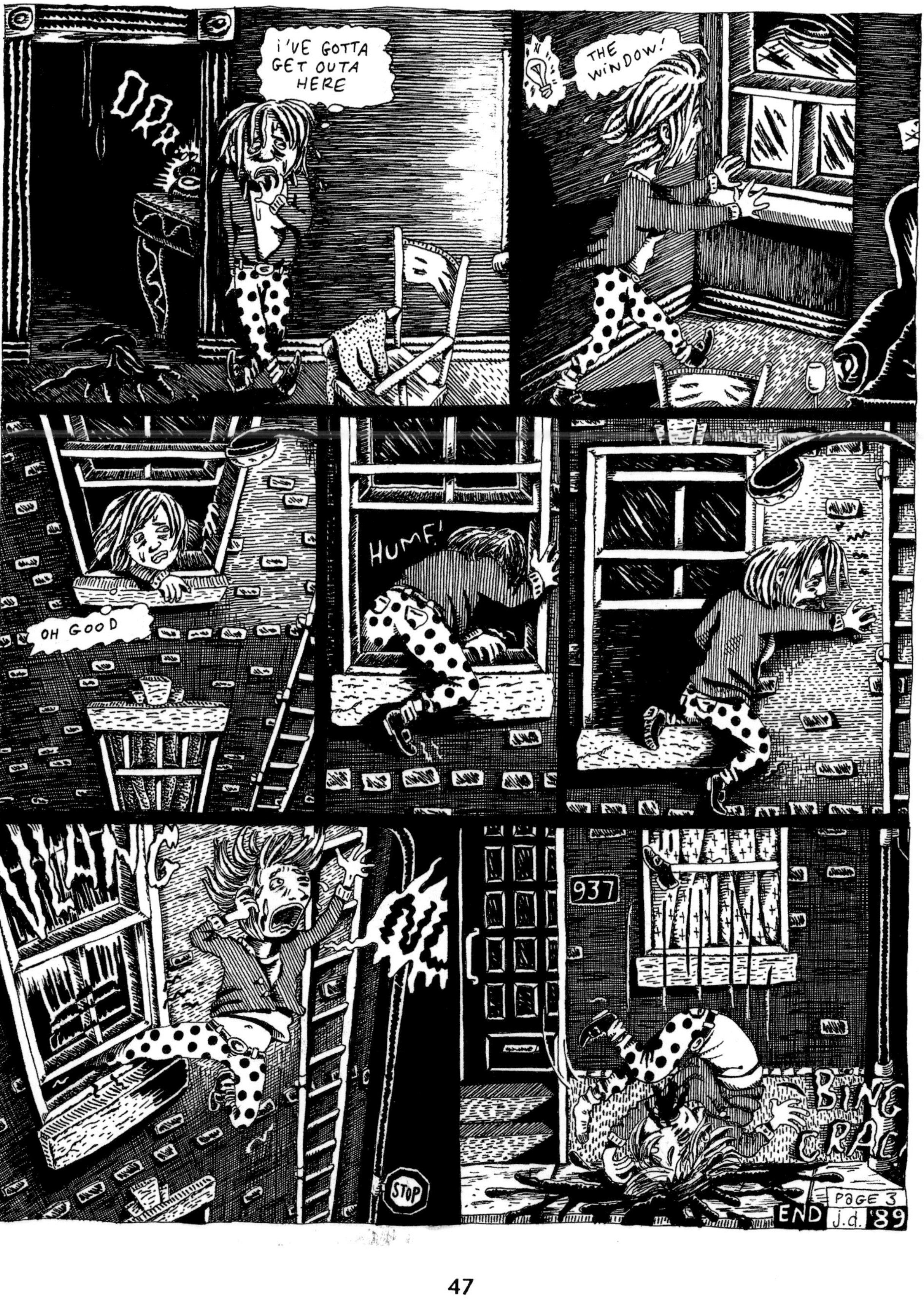
I'VE GOTTA GET OUTA HERE
THE WINDOW!
OH GOOD
HUMF!
937
STOP
BING
CRAC
PAGE 3
END
J.d. '89

Jate

Saposcat gets up one day as usual...

makes a pee...

drinks his coffee...

and going down stairs begins the daily chore of getting to work.

Downstairs he peeks through a crack in the concierge's door at the concierge's daughter.

after which he goes out into the street.

As he crosses the street he realizes, too late, that a car is bearing down on him...

MOOC!

trying to avoid the car he slips and hits his head.

PLONC

He first blames it all on his usual bad luck, but then wonders whether if he hadn't stopped to spy on the concierge's daughter, he wouldn't have suffered the consequences he did,

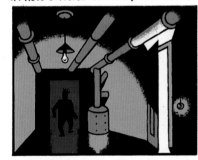

attributing his fall to who knows what evil forces out to get him.

However, a distant bell rings in the back of his mind...

TIN!

Sapo thinks back and realizes that if he hadn't got up just a little later that morning..

he would have taken the time to wash his face and, by so doing, he would have unbeknowingly been disfigured and left blind for life,

since, as he will read in the papers to-morrow, a leak from the nuclear power station next to his apartment building has contaminated all the water in the area...

and, something that Sapo can't know, if he hadn't slipped he would have carried on down the street...

and that, as he crossed again in his usual absent-minded fashion, Sapo would not have noticed a truck full of toxic waste heading straight for him...

and that by trying to avoid him the truck would go out of control and overturn,

thus causing a great many injuries and deaths, Sapo's among them, not to mention the obvious ecological disaster.

Looking at it from this point of view, Sapo, lying on the ground nursing a bad headache, realizes that his luck is not so bad after all,

even if it were entirely possible that he could have got to work without anything at all happening to him.

Although, on the other hand, if he had continued on the same side of the street...

he would, quite by chance as is always the case in matters of the heart, have made the acquaintance of the woman with whom he would fall madly in love and with whom he would share his innermost secrets.

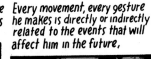

However, the good news about Sapo's love life pales a bit since, after being married for years, he goes off his head,

and ends up murdering his wife and three children before committing suicide.

Such speculations keep Sapo lying there on the ground as he thinks that he has found the "Truth" with a capital T.

Every movement, every gesture he makes is directly or indirectly related to the events that will affect him in the future,

including a very distant future in which his mental gyrations become increasingly demented and uncontrolable.

Sapo doesn't move an eyelid as he considers carefully what action he should take from this moment on in view of what might happen as a consequence.

That's the very moment when the ambulance men take Sapo off, believing him to be completely paralysed, while he continues to speculate...

49

fin.

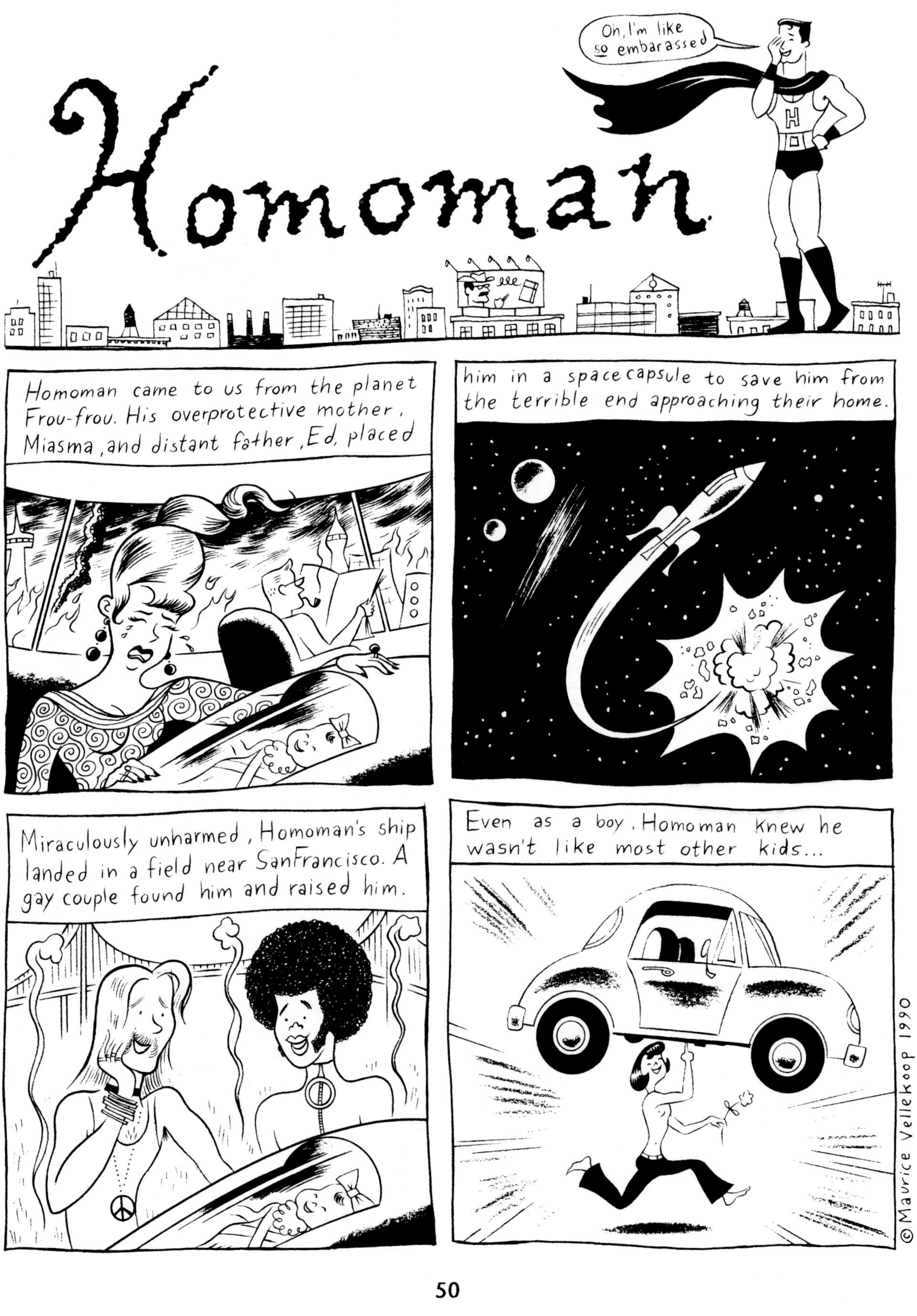
Oh, I'm like so embarassed
Homoman
Homoman came to us from the planet Frou-frou. His overprotective mother, Miasma, and distant father, Ed, placed
him in a spacecapsule to save him from the terrible end approaching their home.
Miraculously unharmed, Homoman's ship landed in a field near SanFrancisco. A gay couple found him and raised him.
Even as a boy, Homoman knew he wasn't like most other kids...
© Maurice Vellekoop 1990

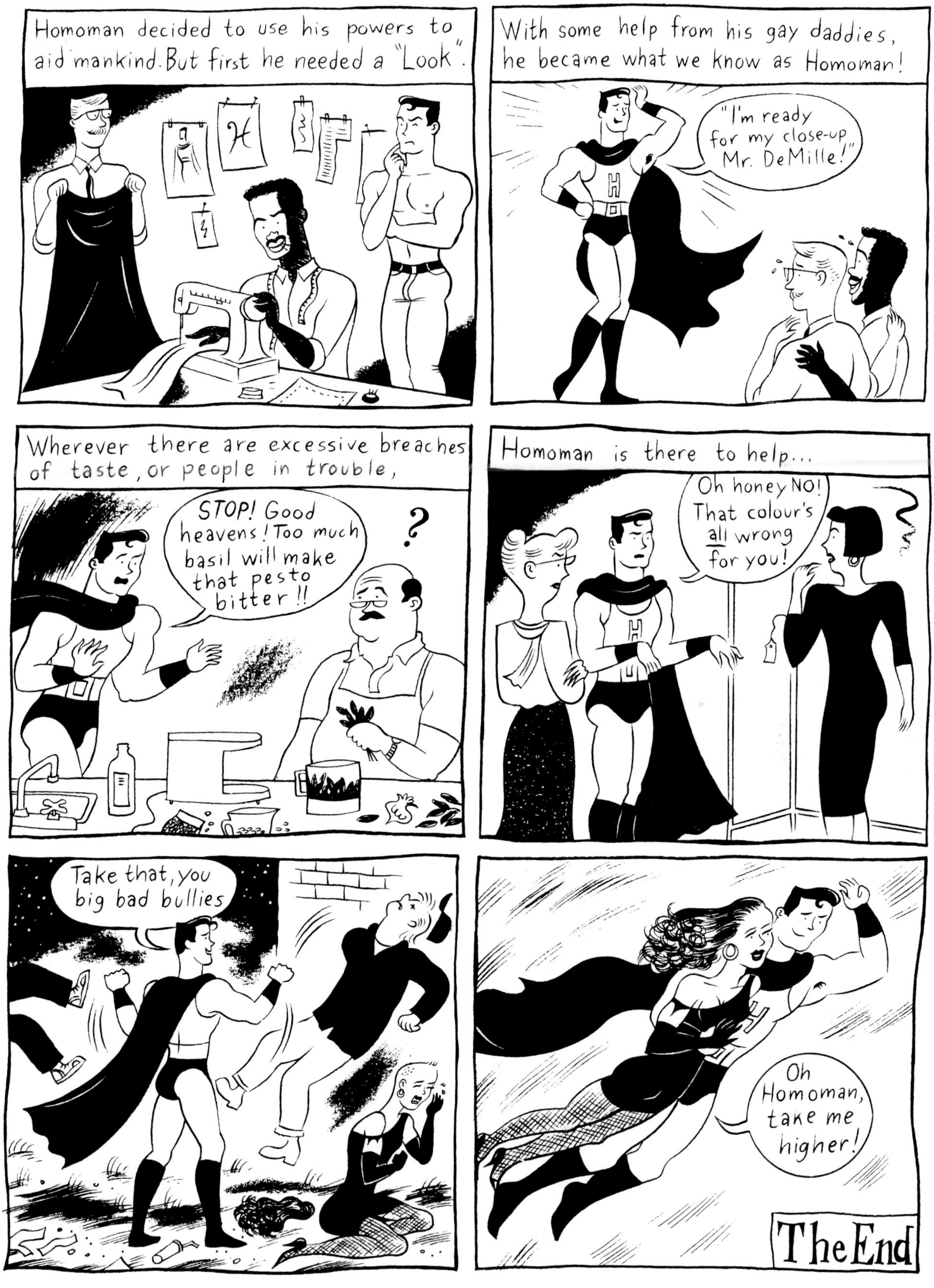
Homoman decided to use his powers to aid mankind. But first he needed a "Look".
With some help from his gay daddies, he became what we know as Homoman!
"I'm ready for my close-up Mr. DeMille!"
Wherever there are excessive breaches of taste, or people in trouble,
STOP! Good heavens! Too much basil will make that pesto bitter!!
?
Homoman is there to help...
Oh honey NO! That colour's all wrong for you!
Take that, you big bad bullies
Oh Homoman, take me higher!
The End

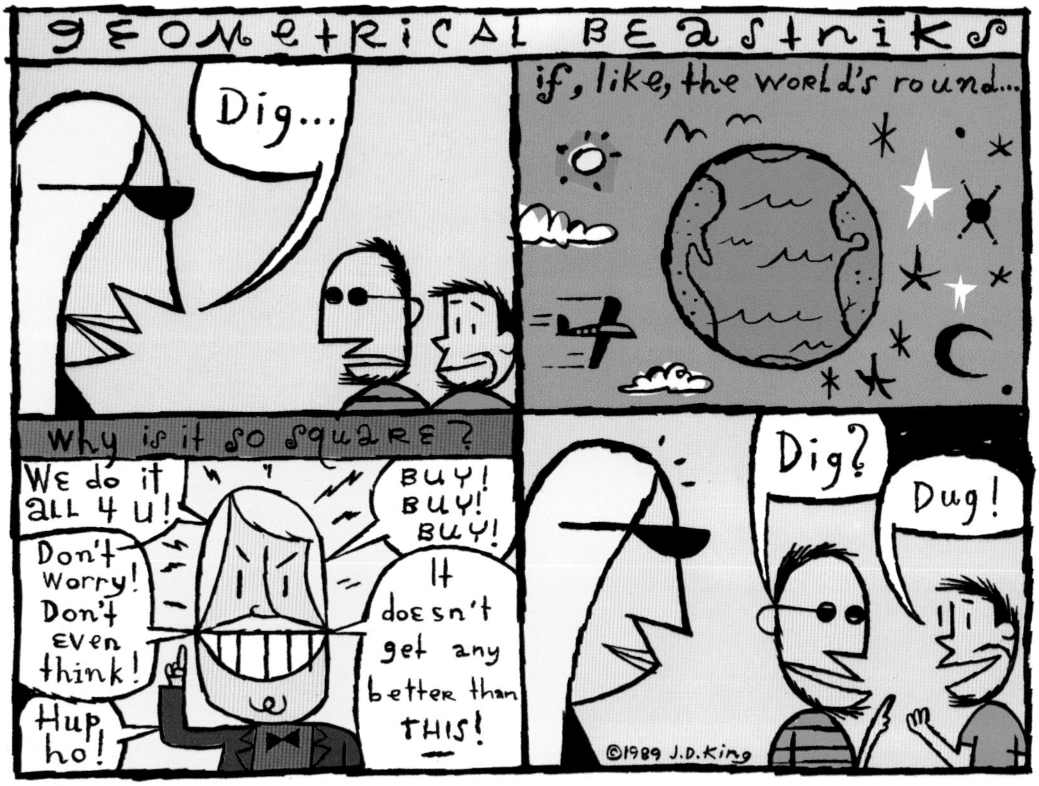
GEOMETRICAL BEASTNIKS
Dig...
if, like, the world's round...
Why is it so square?
We do it all 4 u!
BUY! BUY! BUY!
Don't worry! Don't even think!
It doesn't get any better than THIS!
Hup ho!
Dig?
Dug!
©1989 J.D.King

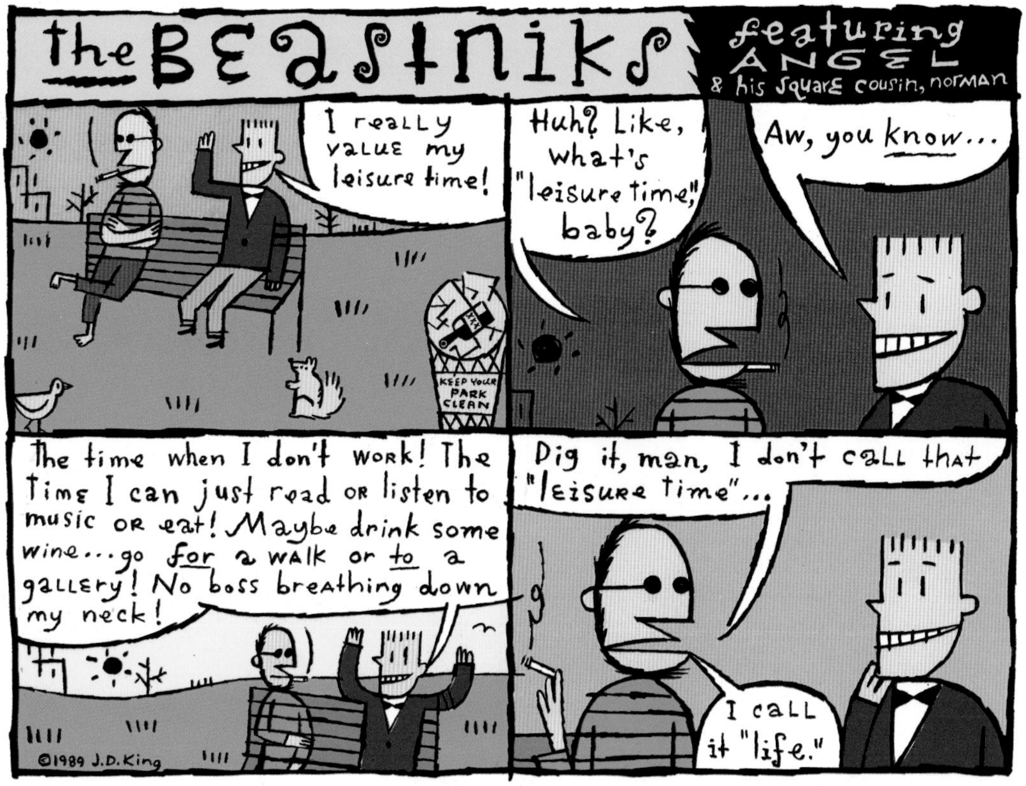
the BEASTNIKS
featuring ANGEL & his square cousin, norman
I really value my leisure time!
KEEP YOUR PARK CLEAN
Huh? Like, what's "leisure time," baby?
Aw, you know...
The time when I don't work! The time I can just read or listen to music or eat! Maybe drink some wine...go for a walk or to a gallery! No boss breathing down my neck!
©1989 J.D.King
Dig it, man, I don't call that "leisure time"...
I call it "life."

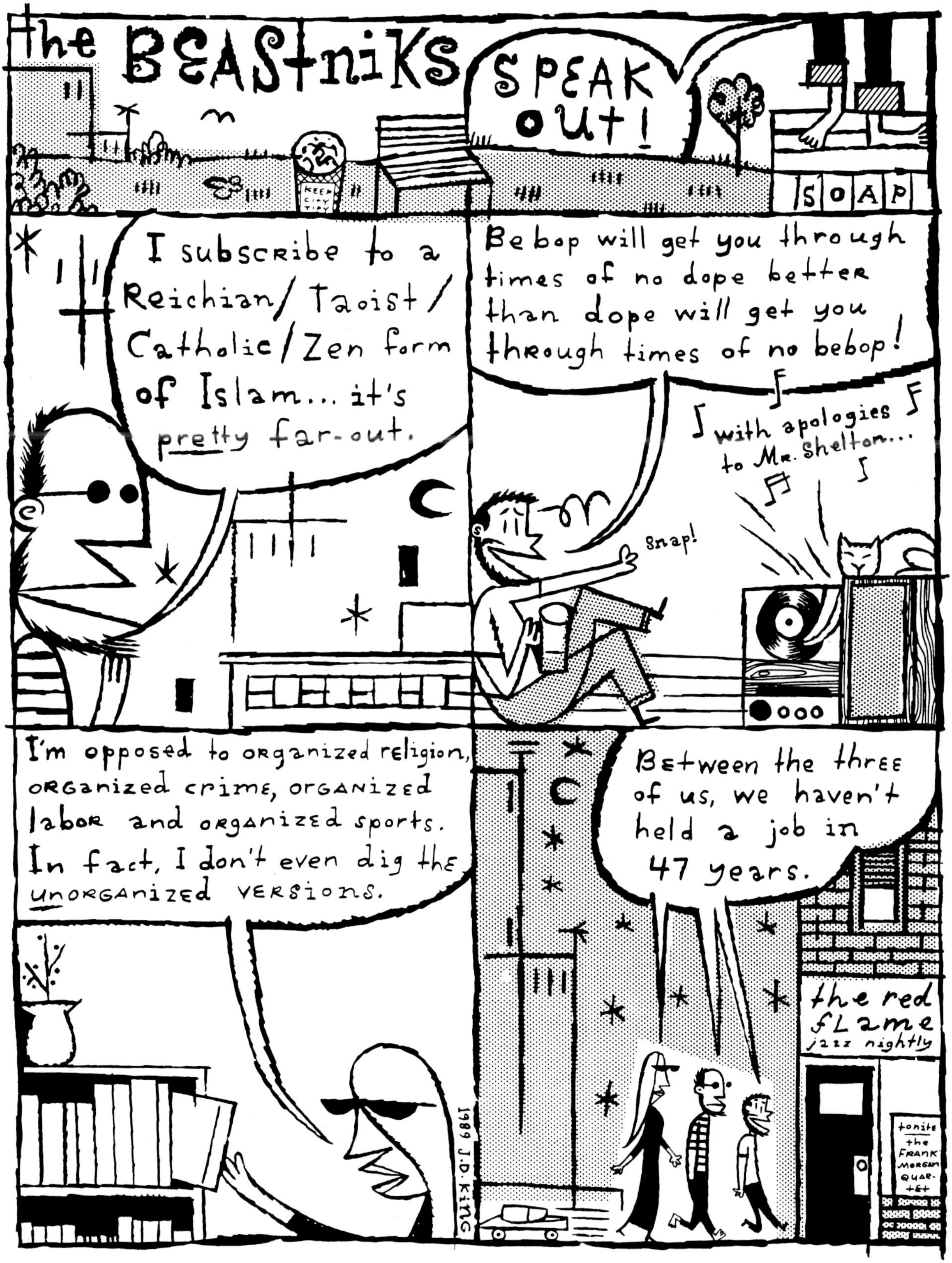

the BEAStniks
SPEAK OUT!
KEEP CITY
SOAP
I subscribe to a Reichian/Taoist/Catholic/Zen form of Islam... it's pretty far-out.
Bebop will get you through times of no dope better than dope will get you through times of no bebop!
with apologies to Mr. Shelton...
Snap!
I'm opposed to organized religion, organized crime, organized labor and organized sports. In fact, I don't even dig the unorganized versions.
1989 J.D. King
Between the three of us, we haven't held a job in 47 years.
the red flame jazz nightly
tonite the FRANK MORGAN QUARTET

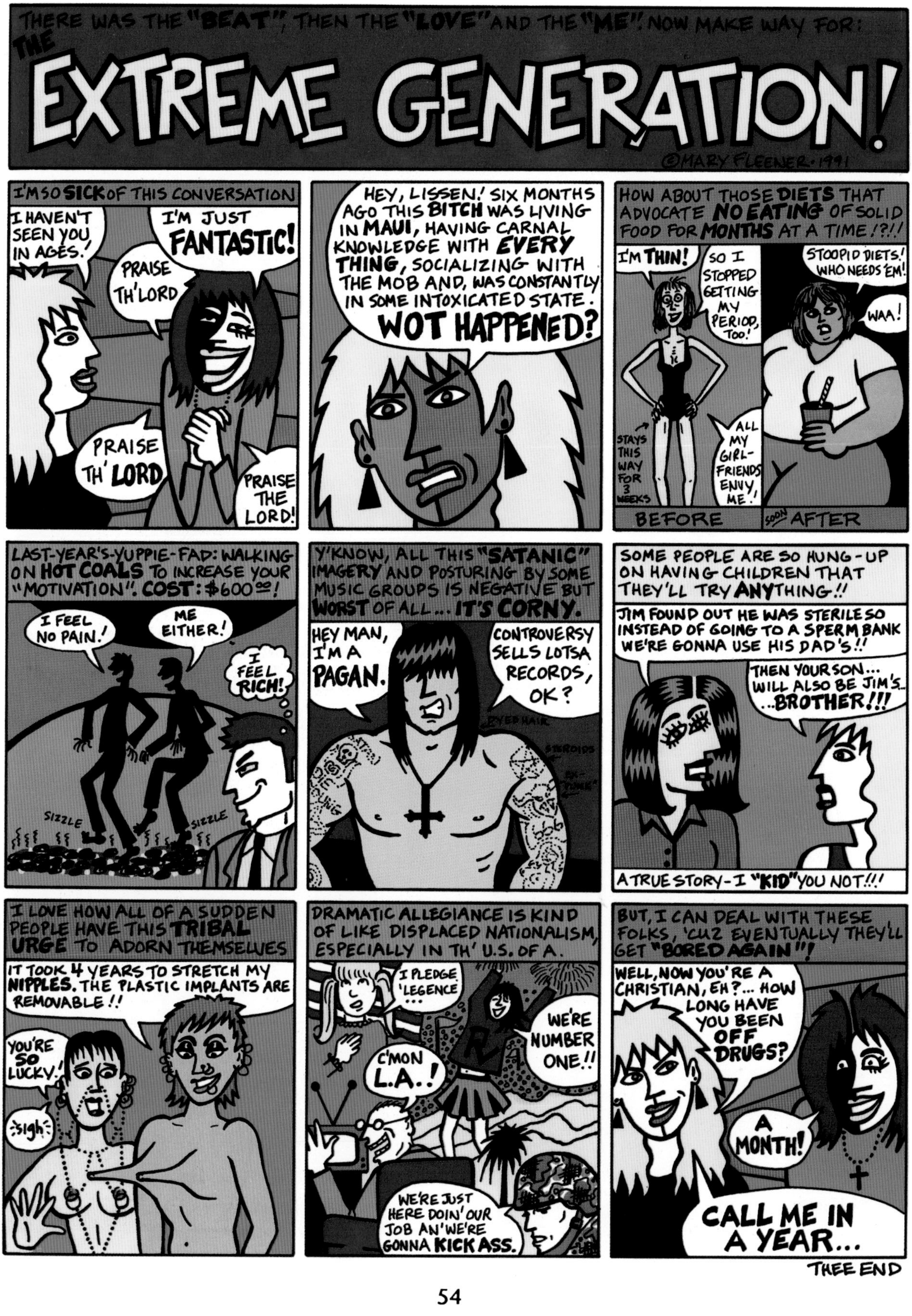
THERE WAS THE "BEAT", THEN THE "LOVE" AND THE "ME". NOW MAKE WAY FOR:
THE EXTREME GENERATION!
©MARY FLEENER·1991
I'M SO SICK OF THIS CONVERSATION
I HAVEN'T SEEN YOU IN AGES!
I'M JUST FANTASTIC!
PRAISE TH'LORD
PRAISE TH' LORD
PRAISE THE LORD!
HEY, LISSEN! SIX MONTHS AGO THIS BITCH WAS LIVING IN MAUI, HAVING CARNAL KNOWLEDGE WITH EVERY THING, SOCIALIZING WITH THE MOB AND, WAS CONSTANTLY IN SOME INTOXICATED STATE. WOT HAPPENED?
HOW ABOUT THOSE DIETS THAT ADVOCATE NO EATING OF SOLID FOOD FOR MONTHS AT A TIME!?!!
I'M THIN!
SO I STOPPED GETTING MY PERIOD, TOO!
ALL MY GIRL-FRIENDS ENVY ME!
STAYS THIS WAY FOR 3 WEEKS
STOOPID DIETS! WHO NEEDS 'EM!
WAA!
BEFORE
SOON AFTER
LAST-YEAR'S-YUPPIE-FAD: WALKING ON HOT COALS TO INCREASE YOUR "MOTIVATION". COST: $600.00!
I FEEL NO PAIN!
ME EITHER!
I FEEL RICH!
SIZZLE
SIZZLE
Y'KNOW, ALL THIS "SATANIC" IMAGERY AND POSTURING BY SOME MUSIC GROUPS IS NEGATIVE BUT WORST OF ALL... IT'S CORNY.
HEY MAN, I'M A PAGAN.
CONTROVERSY SELLS LOTSA RECORDS, OK?
DYED HAIR
STEROIDS
SOME PEOPLE ARE SO HUNG-UP ON HAVING CHILDREN THAT THEY'LL TRY ANYTHING!!
JIM FOUND OUT HE WAS STERILE SO INSTEAD OF GOING TO A SPERM BANK WE'RE GONNA USE HIS DAD'S!!
THEN YOUR SON... WILL ALSO BE JIM'S... ...BROTHER!!!
A TRUE STORY - I "KID" YOU NOT!!!
I LOVE HOW ALL OF A SUDDEN PEOPLE HAVE THIS TRIBAL URGE TO ADORN THEMSELVES
IT TOOK 4 YEARS TO STRETCH MY NIPPLES. THE PLASTIC IMPLANTS ARE REMOVABLE!!
YOU'RE SO LUCKY!
sigh
DRAMATIC ALLEGIANCE IS KIND OF LIKE DISPLACED NATIONALISM, ESPECIALLY IN TH' U.S. OF A.
I PLEDGE 'LEGENCE...
WE'RE NUMBER ONE!!
C'MON L.A.!
WE'RE JUST HERE DOIN' OUR JOB AN' WE'RE GONNA KICK ASS.
BUT, I CAN DEAL WITH THESE FOLKS, 'CUZ EVENTUALLY THEY'LL GET "BORED AGAIN"!
WELL, NOW YOU'RE A CHRISTIAN, EH?... HOW LONG HAVE YOU BEEN OFF DRUGS?
A MONTH!
CALL ME IN A YEAR...
THEE END

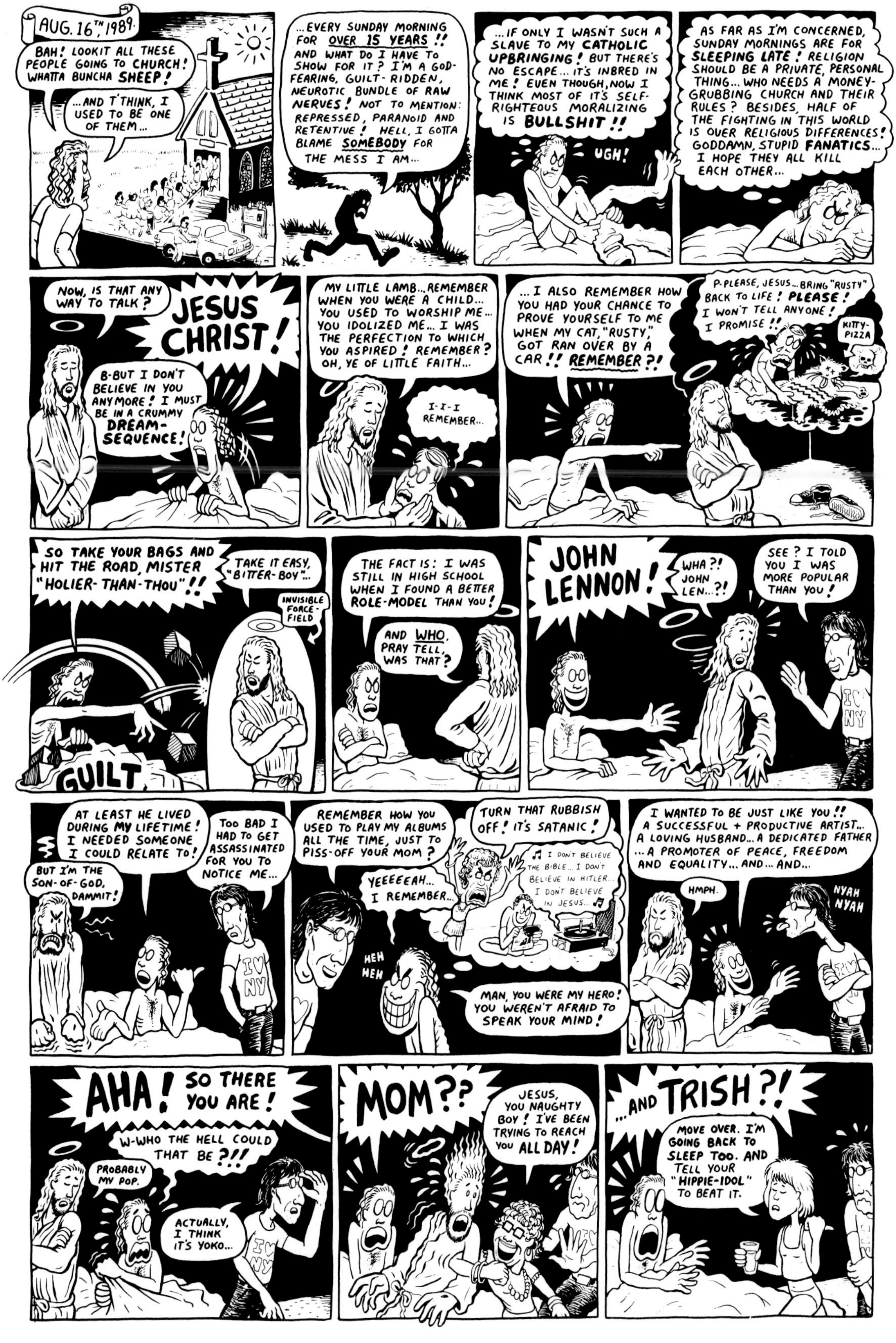
AUG. 16TH, 1989.
BAH! LOOKIT ALL THESE PEOPLE GOING TO CHURCH! WHATTA BUNCHA SHEEP!
...AND T'THINK, I USED TO BE ONE OF THEM...
...EVERY SUNDAY MORNING FOR OVER 15 YEARS!! AND WHAT DO I HAVE TO SHOW FOR IT? I'M A GOD-FEARING, GUILT-RIDDEN, NEUROTIC BUNDLE OF RAW NERVES! NOT TO MENTION: REPRESSED, PARANOID AND RETENTIVE! HELL, I GOTTA BLAME SOMEBODY FOR THE MESS I AM...
...IF ONLY I WASN'T SUCH A SLAVE TO MY CATHOLIC UPBRINGING! BUT THERE'S NO ESCAPE... IT'S INBRED IN ME! EVEN THOUGH, NOW I THINK MOST OF IT'S SELF-RIGHTEOUS MORALIZING IS BULLSHIT!!
UGH!
AS FAR AS I'M CONCERNED, SUNDAY MORNINGS ARE FOR SLEEPING LATE! RELIGION SHOULD BE A PRIVATE, PERSONAL THING... WHO NEEDS A MONEY-GRUBBING CHURCH AND THEIR RULES? BESIDES, HALF OF THE FIGHTING IN THIS WORLD IS OVER RELIGIOUS DIFFERENCES! GODDAMN, STUPID FANATICS... I HOPE THEY ALL KILL EACH OTHER...
NOW, IS THAT ANY WAY TO TALK?
JESUS CHRIST!
B-BUT I DON'T BELIEVE IN YOU ANYMORE! I MUST BE IN A CRUMMY DREAM-SEQUENCE!
MY LITTLE LAMB... REMEMBER WHEN YOU WERE A CHILD... YOU USED TO WORSHIP ME... YOU IDOLIZED ME... I WAS THE PERFECTION TO WHICH YOU ASPIRED! REMEMBER? OH, YE OF LITTLE FAITH...
I-I-I REMEMBER...
...I ALSO REMEMBER HOW YOU HAD YOUR CHANCE TO PROVE YOURSELF TO ME WHEN MY CAT, "RUSTY," GOT RAN OVER BY A CAR!! REMEMBER?!
P-PLEASE, JESUS... BRING "RUSTY" BACK TO LIFE! PLEASE! I WON'T TELL ANYONE! I PROMISE!!
KITTY-PIZZA
SO TAKE YOUR BAGS AND HIT THE ROAD, MISTER "HOLIER-THAN-THOU"!!
TAKE IT EASY, "BITTER-BOY"...
INVISIBLE FORCE-FIELD
GUILT
THE FACT IS: I WAS STILL IN HIGH SCHOOL WHEN I FOUND A BETTER ROLE-MODEL THAN YOU!
AND WHO, PRAY TELL, WAS THAT?
JOHN LENNON!
WHA?! JOHN LEN...?!
SEE? I TOLD YOU I WAS MORE POPULAR THAN YOU!
I ♡ NY
AT LEAST HE LIVED DURING MY LIFETIME! I NEEDED SOMEONE I COULD RELATE TO!
TOO BAD I HAD TO GET ASSASSINATED FOR YOU TO NOTICE ME...
BUT I'M THE SON-OF-GOD, DAMMIT!
REMEMBER HOW YOU USED TO PLAY MY ALBUMS ALL THE TIME, JUST TO PISS-OFF YOUR MOM?
TURN THAT RUBBISH OFF! IT'S SATANIC!
♫ I DON'T BELIEVE THE BIBLE... I DON'T BELIEVE IN HITLER... I DON'T BELIEVE IN JESUS... ♫
YEEEEEAH... I REMEMBER...
HEH HEH
MAN, YOU WERE MY HERO! YOU WEREN'T AFRAID TO SPEAK YOUR MIND!
I WANTED TO BE JUST LIKE YOU!! A SUCCESSFUL + PRODUCTIVE ARTIST... A LOVING HUSBAND... A DEDICATED FATHER ...A PROMOTER OF PEACE, FREEDOM AND EQUALITY... AND... AND...
HMPH.
NYAH NYAH
AHA! SO THERE YOU ARE!
W-WHO THE HELL COULD THAT BE?!!
PROBABLY MY POP.
ACTUALLY, I THINK IT'S YOKO...
MOM??
JESUS, YOU NAUGHTY BOY! I'VE BEEN TRYING TO REACH YOU ALL DAY!
...AND TRISH?!
MOVE OVER. I'M GOING BACK TO SLEEP TOO. AND TELL YOUR "HIPPIE-IDOL" TO BEAT IT.

MUSIC

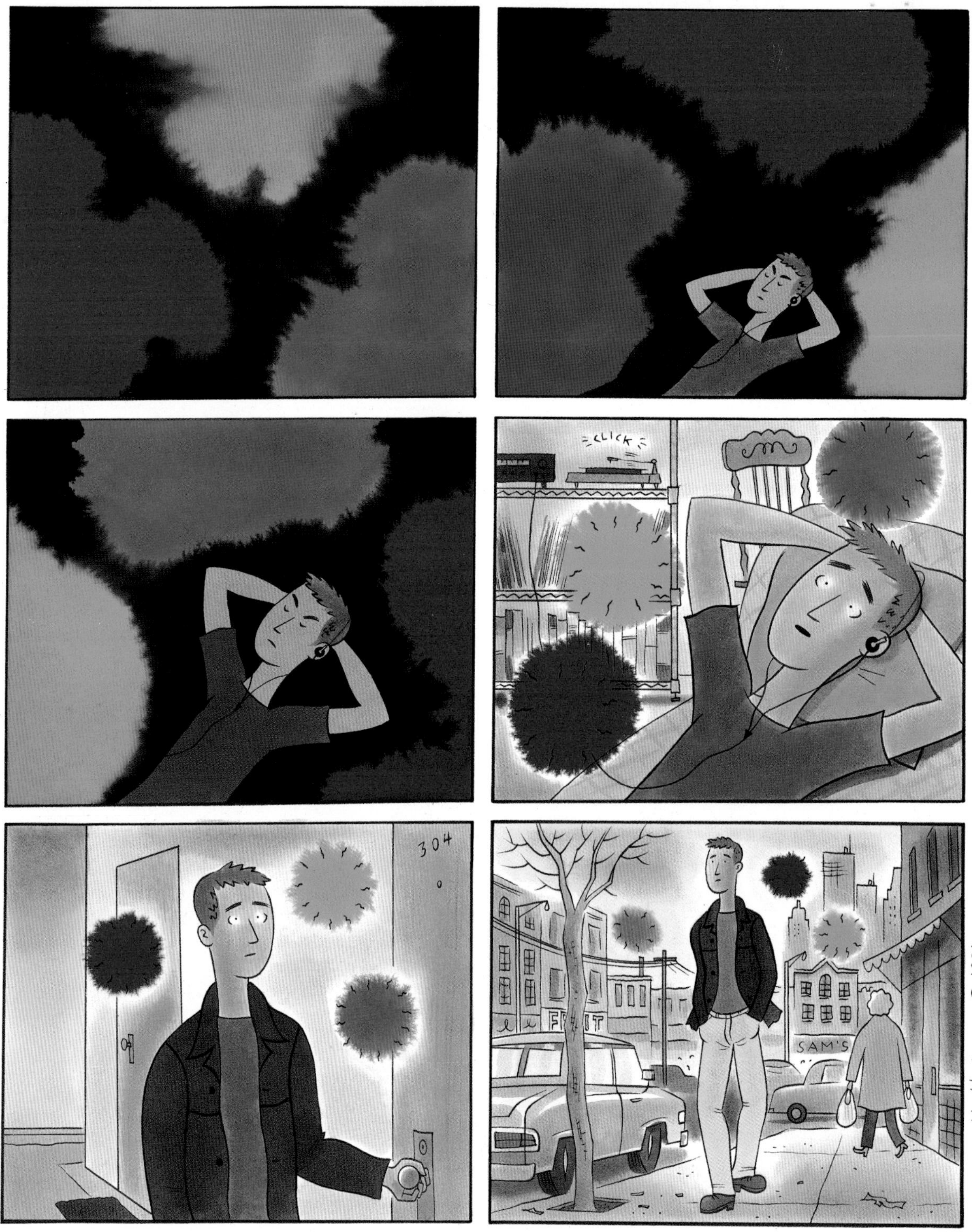
CLICK
304
FRUIT
SAM'S

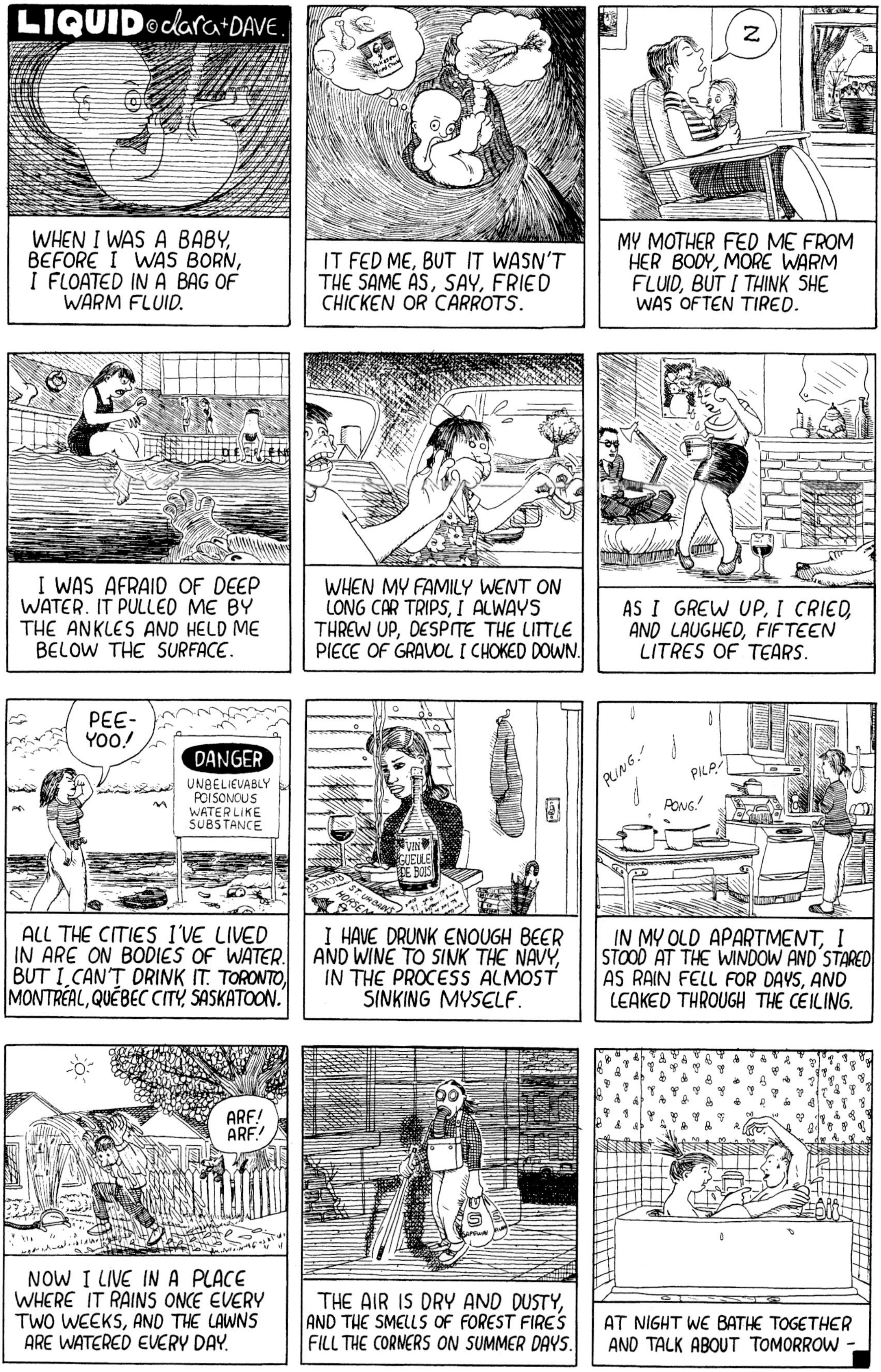
LIQUID © clara+DAVE.
WHEN I WAS A BABY, BEFORE I WAS BORN, I FLOATED IN A BAG OF WARM FLUID.
IT FED ME, BUT IT WASN'T THE SAME AS, SAY, FRIED CHICKEN OR CARROTS.
Z
MY MOTHER FED ME FROM HER BODY, MORE WARM FLUID, BUT I THINK SHE WAS OFTEN TIRED.
I WAS AFRAID OF DEEP WATER. IT PULLED ME BY THE ANKLES AND HELD ME BELOW THE SURFACE.
WHEN MY FAMILY WENT ON LONG CAR TRIPS, I ALWAYS THREW UP, DESPITE THE LITTLE PIECE OF GRAVOL I CHOKED DOWN.
AS I GREW UP, I CRIED, AND LAUGHED, FIFTEEN LITRES OF TEARS.
PEE-YOO!
DANGER
UNBELIEVABLY POISONOUS WATERLIKE SUBSTANCE
ALL THE CITIES I'VE LIVED IN ARE ON BODIES OF WATER. BUT I CAN'T DRINK IT. TORONTO, MONTRÉAL, QUÉBEC CITY, SASKATOON.
VIN GUEULE DE BOIS
I HAVE DRUNK ENOUGH BEER AND WINE TO SINK THE NAVY, IN THE PROCESS ALMOST SINKING MYSELF.
PLING!
PILP!
PONG!
IN MY OLD APARTMENT, I STOOD AT THE WINDOW AND STARED AS RAIN FELL FOR DAYS, AND LEAKED THROUGH THE CEILING.
ARF! ARF!
NOW I LIVE IN A PLACE WHERE IT RAINS ONCE EVERY TWO WEEKS, AND THE LAWNS ARE WATERED EVERY DAY.
THE AIR IS DRY AND DUSTY, AND THE SMELLS OF FOREST FIRES FILL THE CORNERS ON SUMMER DAYS.
AT NIGHT WE BATHE TOGETHER AND TALK ABOUT TOMORROW -

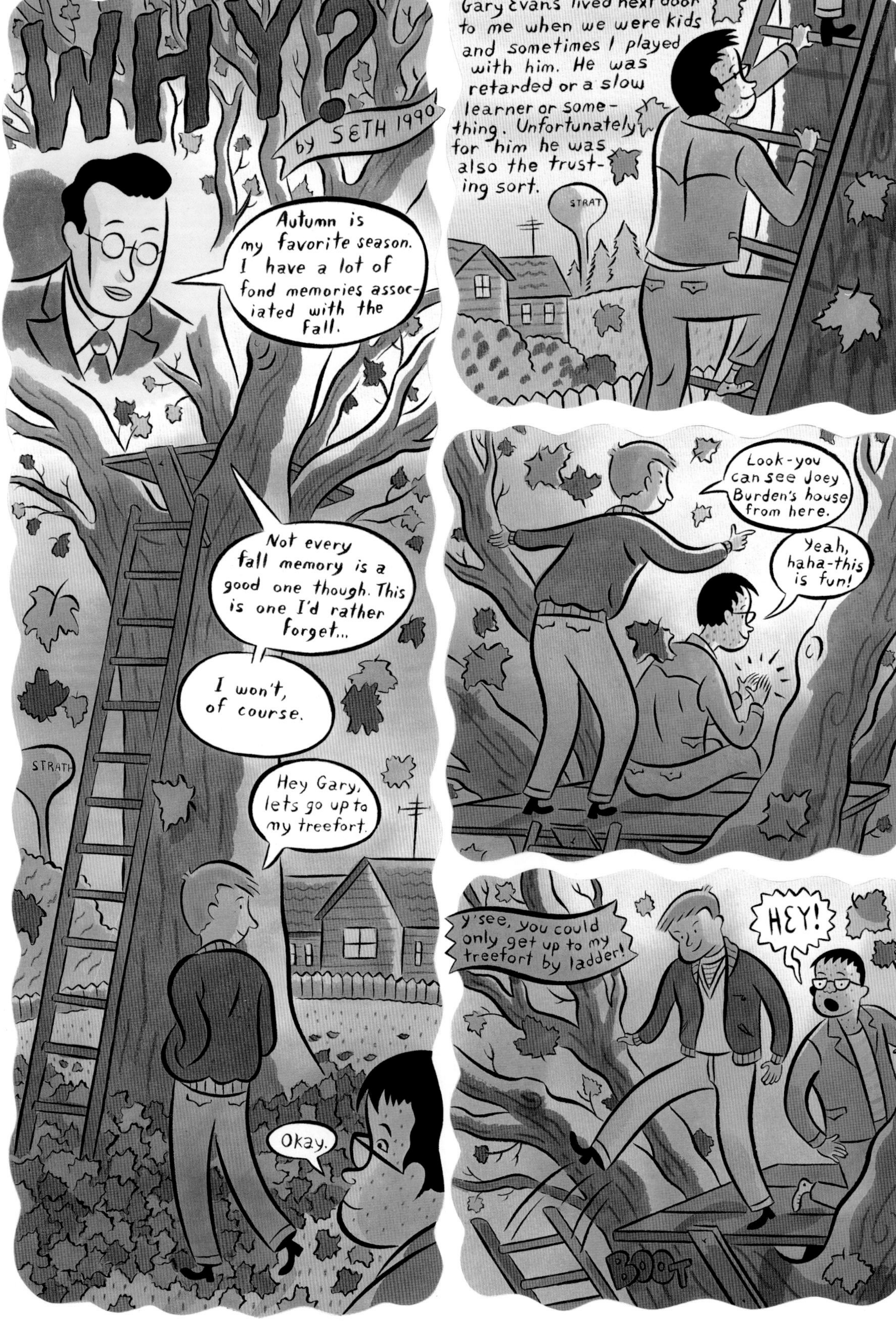
WHY?
by SETH 1990
Autumn is my favorite season. I have a lot of fond memories associated with the fall.
Not every fall memory is a good one though. This is one I'd rather forget...
I won't, of course.
STRATH
Hey Gary, lets go up to my treefort.
Okay.
Gary Evans lived next door to me when we were kids and sometimes I played with him. He was retarded or a slow learner or something. Unfortunately for him he was also the trusting sort.
STRAT
Look-you can see Joey Burden's house from here.
Yeah, haha-this is fun!
y'see, you could only get up to my treefort by ladder!
HEY!
BOOT

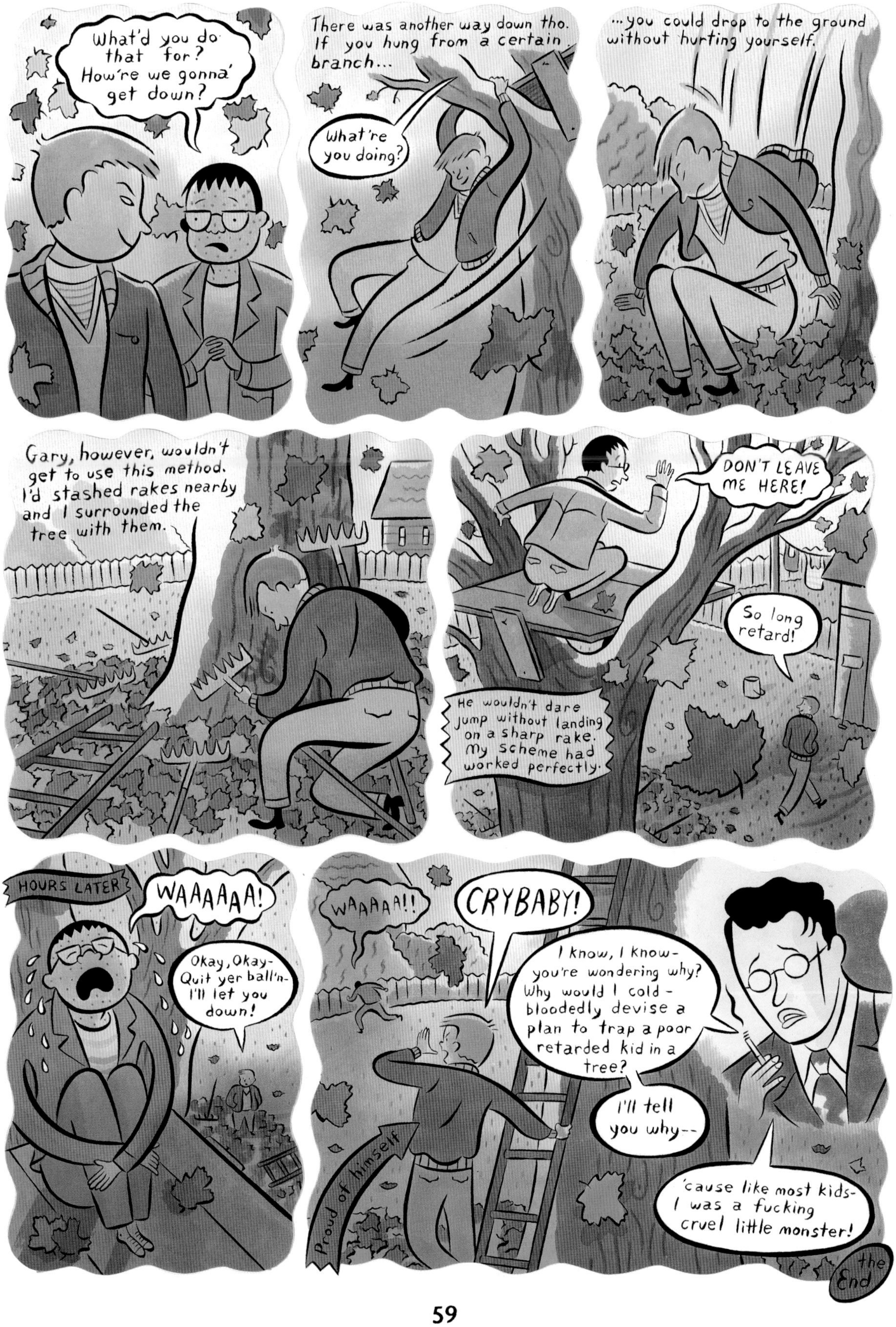
What'd you do that for? How're we gonna' get down?
There was another way down tho. If you hung from a certain branch...
What're you doing?
...you could drop to the ground without hurting yourself.
Gary, however, wouldn't get to use this method. I'd stashed rakes nearby and I surrounded the tree with them.
DON'T LEAVE ME HERE!
So long retard!
He wouldn't dare jump without landing on a sharp rake. My scheme had worked perfectly.
HOURS LATER
WAAAAAA!
Okay, Okay- Quit yer ball'n- I'll let you down!
WAAAAA!!
CRYBABY!
I know, I know- you're wondering why? Why would I cold-bloodedly devise a plan to trap a poor retarded kid in a tree?
I'll tell you why--
Proud of himself
'cause like most kids- I was a fucking cruel little monster!
the End

A DEAR JOHN LETTER FROM YOUR DOG ON MOVING DAY

written by Philip Fine drawn by John Oliveros

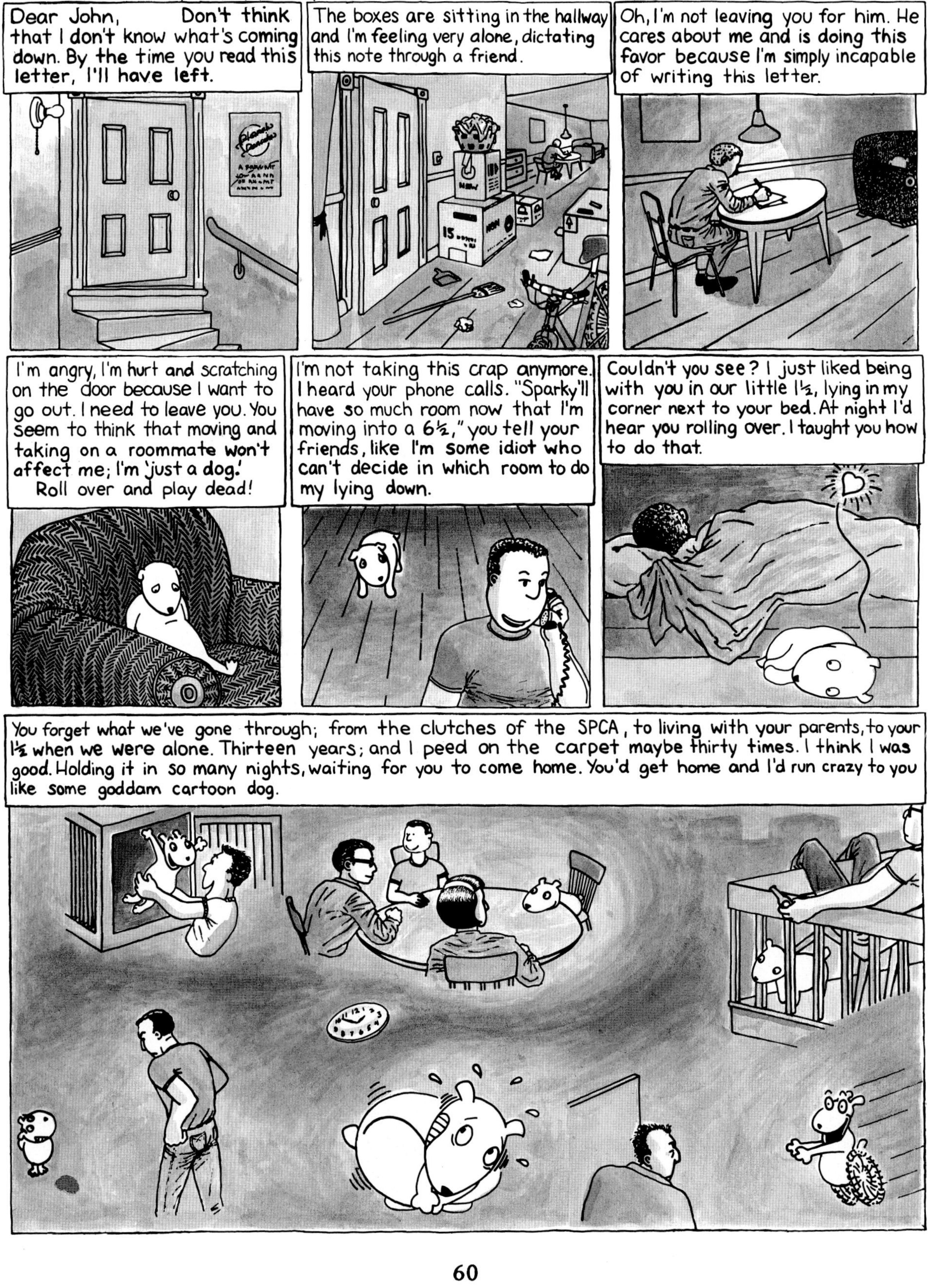
Dear John, Don't think that I don't know what's coming down. By the time you read this letter, I'll have left.
The boxes are sitting in the hallway and I'm feeling very alone, dictating this note through a friend.
Oh, I'm not leaving you for him. He cares about me and is doing this favor because I'm simply incapable of writing this letter.
I'm angry, I'm hurt and scratching on the door because I want to go out. I need to leave you. You seem to think that moving and taking on a roommate won't affect me; I'm 'just a dog.' Roll over and play dead!
I'm not taking this crap anymore. I heard your phone calls. "Sparky'll have so much room now that I'm moving into a 6½," you tell your friends, like I'm some idiot who can't decide in which room to do my lying down.
Couldn't you see? I just liked being with you in our little 1½, lying in my corner next to your bed. At night I'd hear you rolling over. I taught you how to do that.
You forget what we've gone through; from the clutches of the SPCA, to living with your parents, to your 1½ when we were alone. Thirteen years; and I peed on the carpet maybe thirty times. I think I was good. Holding it in so many nights, waiting for you to come home. You'd get home and I'd run crazy to you like some goddam cartoon dog.

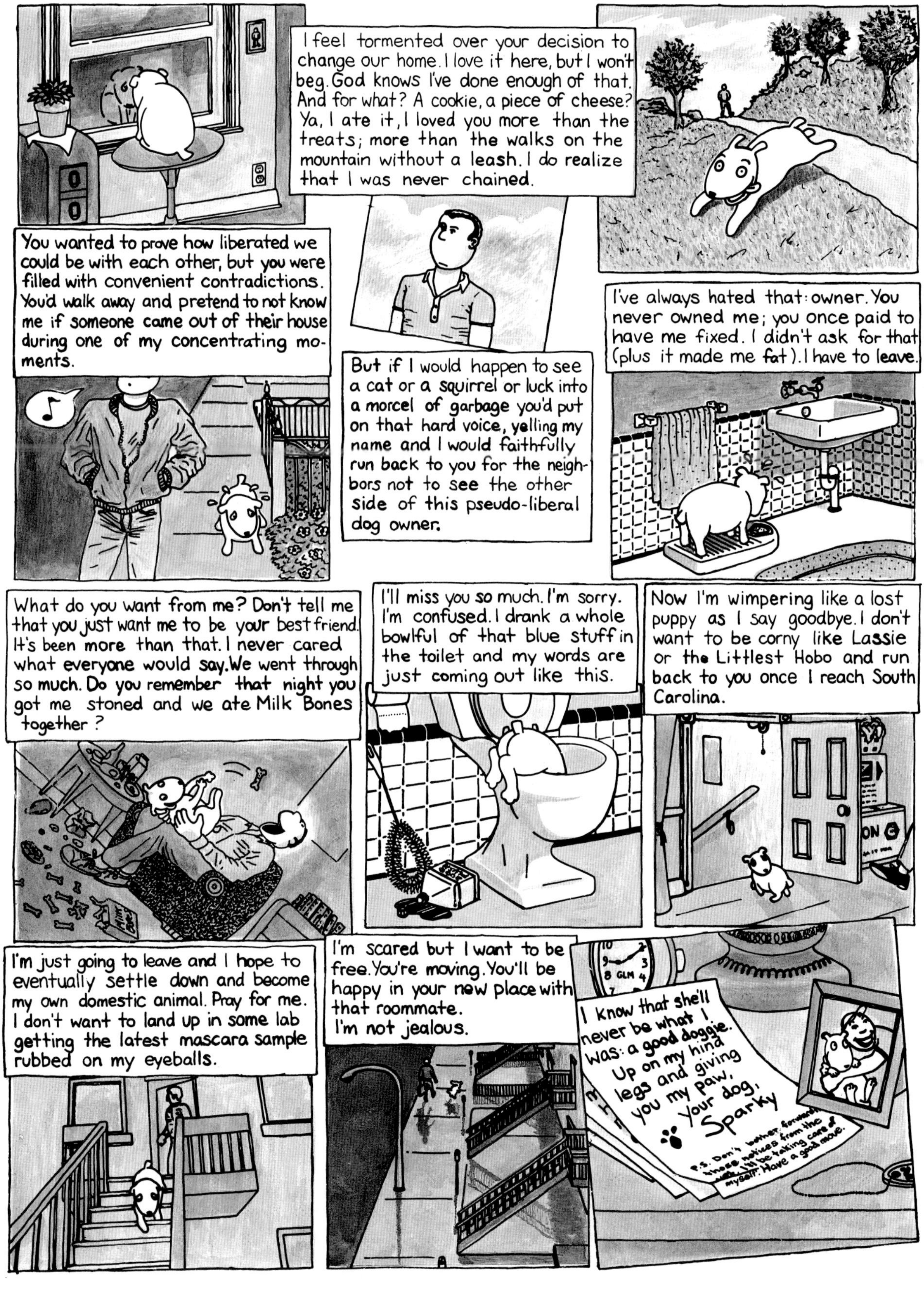
I feel tormented over your decision to change our home. I love it here, but I won't beg. God knows I've done enough of that. And for what? A cookie, a piece of cheese? Ya, I ate it, I loved you more than the treats; more than the walks on the mountain without a leash. I do realize that I was never chained.
You wanted to prove how liberated we could be with each other, but you were filled with convenient contradictions. You'd walk away and pretend to not know me if someone came out of their house during one of my concentrating moments.
But if I would happen to see a cat or a squirrel or luck into a morcel of garbage you'd put on that hard voice, yelling my name and I would faithfully run back to you for the neighbors not to see the other side of this pseudo-liberal dog owner.
I've always hated that: owner. You never owned me; you once paid to have me fixed. I didn't ask for that (plus it made me fat). I have to leave.
What do you want from me? Don't tell me that you just want me to be your best friend. It's been more than that. I never cared what everyone would say. We went through so much. Do you remember that night you got me stoned and we ate Milk Bones together?
I'll miss you so much. I'm sorry. I'm confused. I drank a whole bowlful of that blue stuff in the toilet and my words are just coming out like this.
Now I'm wimpering like a lost puppy as I say goodbye. I don't want to be corny like Lassie or the Littlest Hobo and run back to you once I reach South Carolina.
I'm just going to leave and I hope to eventually settle down and become my own domestic animal. Pray for me. I don't want to land up in some lab getting the latest mascara sample rubbed on my eyeballs.
I'm scared but I want to be free. You're moving. You'll be happy in your new place with that roommate. I'm not jealous.
I know that she'll never be what I was: a good doggie. Up on my hind legs and giving you my paw. Your dog, Sparky
P.S. Don't bother forwarding those notices from the I'll be taking care of myself. Have a good move.

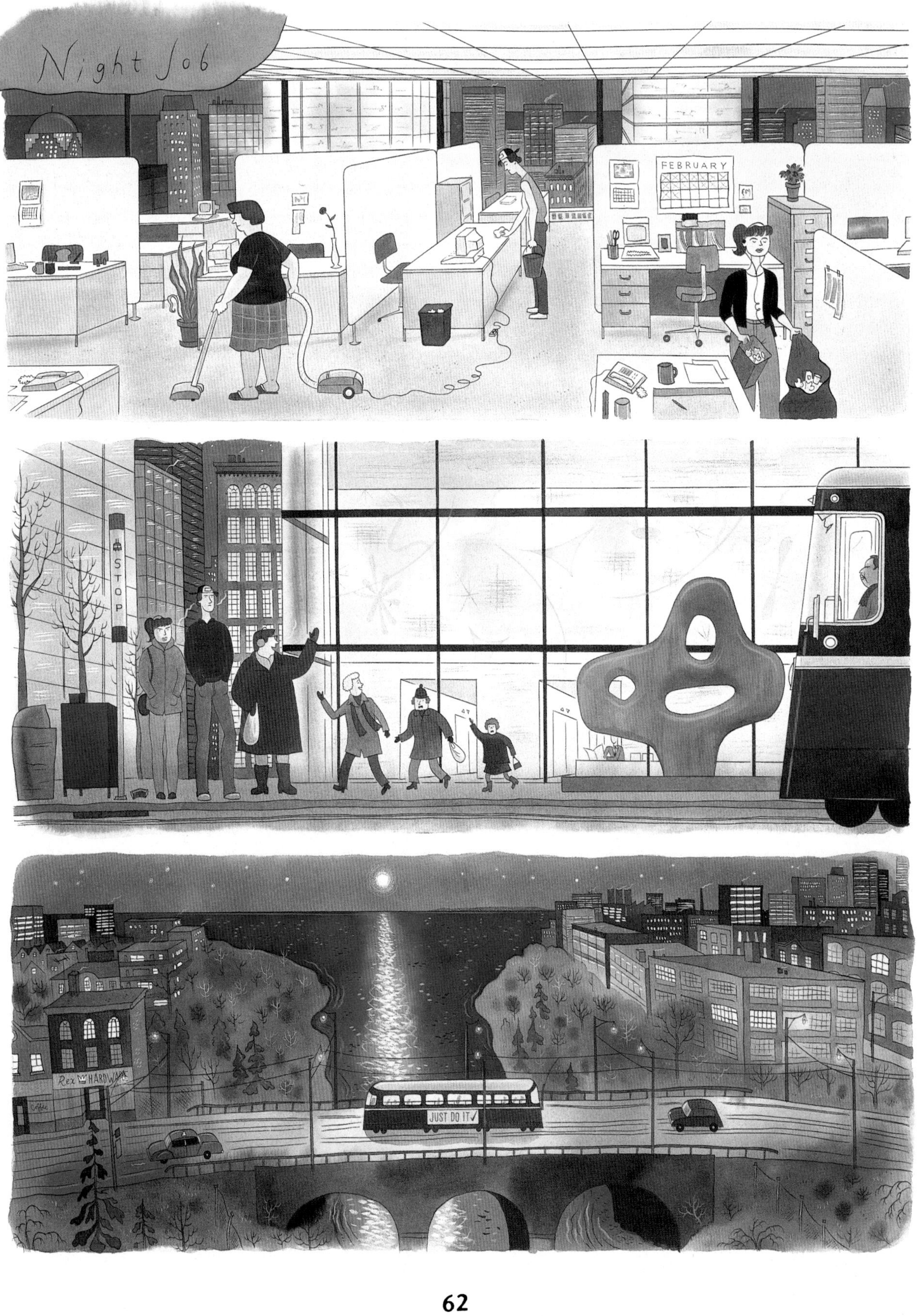
Night Job
FEBRUARY
STOP
JUST DO IT✓

Biographies

- **Santiago Cohen** (pages 2, 24, 40, and 63) is a pathological liar and uses his gift to sometimes create strange stories in which he gives the impression of having an exciting and sophisticated life. He lives in a bird's nest, five minutes from New York and spends as much time as he can with his flea circus.

- **Clara Bayliss-Collier** (story: page 57) used to write strips for her husband David, but now she's busy attending the University of Saskatchewan, where she dreams of becoming a Doctor of Psychology.

- **David Collier's** (art: page 57) comics appear in *The Comics Journal* and his comic series *Collier's*.

- **Julie Doucet's** (pages 39 and 45) new book, the one with the hard-to-pronounce title, has just been published by D&Q. *Lève Ta Jambe, Mon Poisson Est Mort!* collects a selection of her early comics work.

- **Michael Dougan's** (pages 5 and 20) second book, *I Can't Tell You Anything*, was published in 1993 by Viking/Penguin. He's currently working on an animated cartoon, *The Dangwoods*, for MTV's Liquid Television.

- **Debbie Drechsler** (pages 25 and 31) is going through mid-life crisis. She used to think this only happened to Old people, only to find that she has, apparently, become one. Her second story in this book, "Constellations", has the distinction of being only one of two strips printed here that hasn't appeared in any of the first ten issues.

- **Philip Fine** (story: page 60) comes from a loud family. So be glad you're reading this in your voice and not having it read in his. He makes his living trying to get his voice heard as a journalist and playwright.

- **Mary Fleener** (page 54) currently lives and surfs in Encinitas, California where she writes and draws her comic series *Slutburger*. She also does strips and illustrations for *Blab!*, *Weirdo*, *Heavy Metal*, *Entertainment Weekly*, *Spin*, and *The Village Voice*.

- **Luc Giard** (page 44) has been feverishly painting his manic, colourful, and intense images for years. If you're lucky, you might find his work in Amsterdam or Australia. Write to him at: 3405 Place Decelles, Apt. 302, Montreal, Quebec, Canada H3S 1X3

- **Roberta Gregory** (page 21) has been writing and drawing comics for nearly two decades, from strips in early issues of *Wimmen's Comix* and *Gay Comix*, to her current comic series, *Naughty Bits*.

- **J.D. King** (page 52) is a swinger with looks and brains to kill or die for. Outside of that, there isn't much to say.

- **Peter Kuper** (page 38) would rather be galivanting around the world with his wife Betty than just about anything else. His work can be found in *Bleeding Heart*, *World War 3*, and *ComicsTrips*, a sketchbook chronicle of his travels in Africa and South East Asia.

- **Francisco Torres Linhart** (page 48) is a twenty-five-year-old artist from Spain whose all-too-rare comic strips occasionally appear in *El Víbora*.

- **Marti** (pages 16 and 36) was one of a small handful of cartoonists who revitalized Spanish comics about fifteen years ago. In North America, his book *The Cabbie* was published by Catalan and a number of his short stories have appeared in *RAW*.

- **Joe Matt** (pages 17 and 55) is still looking desperately for his ideal, skinny, exotic woman (preferably a fast-walking, tom-boyish, non-smoker) with dark hair, heavy eyebrows, big lips, small breasts, narrow hips, large ears, with a toleration for pornography, and...oh, never mind.

- After a brief but noisy career in super-hero comics, **David Mazzucchelli** (page 22) found his way into the exciting but much quieter world of alternative comics, most notably through his excellent self-published anthology *Rubber Blanket*. He's also a frequent contibutor to *The New Yorker*.

- **Carel Moiseiwitsch** (page 14) has almost given up drawing and taken up learning surfing and arabic. She'll keep us informed as to what kind of career choices open up.

- **John Oliveros** (art: page 60) was looking for something to do when he bumped into Philip Fine, years after they had been in grade six together. The result of their chance meeting was "A Dear John Letter...", originally written as a radio piece.

- **Richard Sala's** (page 4) animated serial *Invisible Hands* has appeared on MTV's Liquid Television. His comics have been collected into two books by Kitchen Sink Press: *Hypnotic Tales* (1992), and *Black Cat Crossing* (1993).

- **Seth** (pages 3, 8, and 58) draws pictures for numerous magazines. He hopes that one day he won't have to come up with those tiny illustrations for those stupid crossword puzzles so that he can finally devote more time to his comic book *Palooka-Ville*.

- **Kate Sibbald** (translations: pages 16, 36, and 48) lives in Montreal where she teaches Spanish literature for a living.

- **Carol Tyler** (page 18) apologizes for leaving out an important component in her profile of Southern Men. "Where was my mind - I left out Football! It's religion to some fellers." Her recent book, *The Job Thing*, is available at fine comic stores.

- **Jet Trash Maurice Vellekoop** (Covers and endpapers; pages 10, 50, 56, and 62) has been to Italy, France, New York, and Germany all in the last year and is wondering whether to go to Paris so he can attend a drag ball. Where he gets the time to draw pictures, I don't know.

- **Dennis Worden** (page 42) has killed off his *Stickboy* series and now edits *Cruel and Unusual Punishment*. At the moment, he's busy working on paintings and *Stickboy* videos.

I thank with all my might the Virgin of the Futile Causes for saving my business after the bus accident from the racoon Convention in Atlantic City.
September 16 1986
Roger the snake Pelskin.

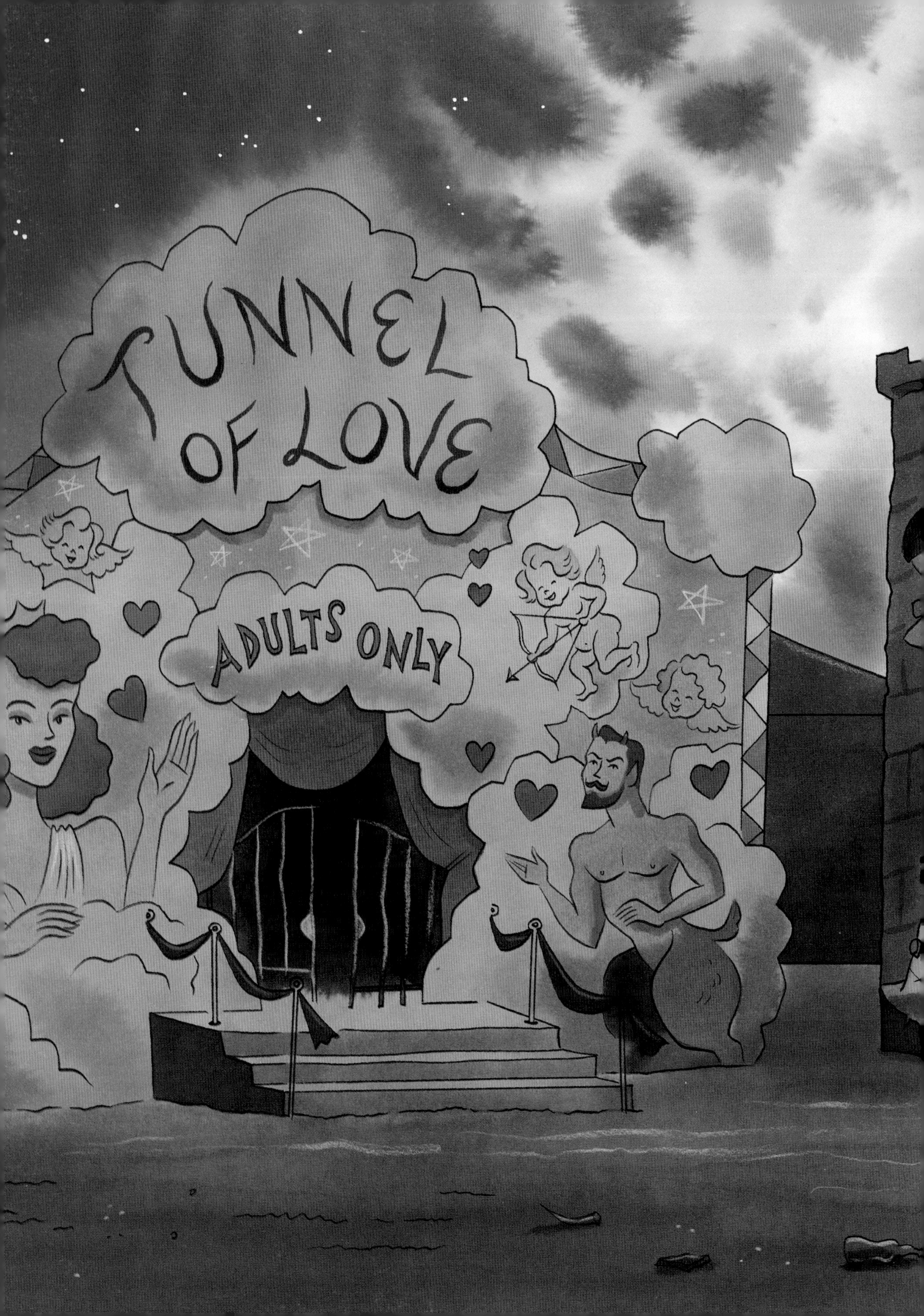
TUNNEL OF LOVE
ADULTS ONLY